CUISINE

ACTUELLE

VICTOR GIELISSE

Certified Master Chef

FOREWORD BY
FERDINAND E. METZ, C.M.C.
**PRESIDENT,
THE CULINARY INSTITUTE
OF AMERICA**

CUISINE
ACTUELLE

TAYLOR PUBLISHING COMPANY
DALLAS, TEXAS

Published by

Taylor Publishing Company
1550 West Mockingbird Lane
Dallas, Texas 75235

Designed by Walter Gray Lamb

Library of Congress Cataloging-in-Publication Data

Gielisse, Victor.
    Cuisine actuelle/Victor Gielisse; foreword by Ferdinand E. Metz.
        p.   cm.
    Includes index.
    ISBN 0-87833-786-5 : $21.95
    1. Cookery.   I. Title.
TX651.G54   1992
641.5—dc20   91-48134   CIP

Printed in the
United States of America

10 9 8 7 6 5 4 3 2 1

◇

In loving memory of my mother, Marion Reichstein Gielisse.

To my father and all my family.

To my wife Kathryn and daughter Marykathryn.

F ew words can describe my gratitude to all the wonderful people who graciously gave their time to make *Cuisine Actuelle* a reality. First and foremost to Taylor Publishing and Mary Kelly who never lost faith in my project from day one. To my editor, Holly McGuire, most gracious, professional, and patient. To Nancy Skodack for her contribution in nutritional analysis, a wonderful person and friend who has taught me so much over the past few years—God bless you, Nancy. To Ferdinand E. Metz for his guidance, encouragement, friendship, and tremendous knowledge in an ever-pressing search to achieve excellence. To a very special friend and colleague, Henri Mahler, pastry chef extraordinaire, for his support, guidance, and knowledge throughout the past ten years that we have been friends. The pastry section in *Cuisine Actuelle* is a direct reflection of the influence Chef Henri has had on my work in that area. Thank you, Henri, for being there for me! A very special thank you to my Sous Chef Kenneth Gladysz, for his loyal support over the past three years and in the long task of testing and perfecting recipes. To *all* my staff who have worked so diligently during the course of this project, especially moving and opening our new restaurant, and who made sure that the work did not lag behind and our guests were first at every turn. To all our regular guests, so many good friends come to mind, thank you for your continued loyalty to our restaurant! To all the photographers for their outstanding work—thank you for your patience and quality work! Thank you to my friends at KraftMaid, Inc., Richard Moody, William Lunte, and Janice Patee, for allowing me to use a photograph from their advertising campaign. To my partner Clive O'Donoghue, thanks for all your support and encouragement over the years and the numerous contributions you have made to my many projects!

And last but not least to you, Kathryn, for putting it all together, line by line, recipe by recipe, word for word, reading my scribbled handwriting, correcting and questioning, and always encouraging, for without your tremendous efforts this would not have come together as it did. To my daughter Marykathryn, for your patience while Mommie and Daddy worked for hours at the computer, never complaining about the time taken away from you in our already hurried daily schedule—I love you!

To all of you, my deepest and sincerest thanks. You are truly leaders and I thank you for your unselfish cooperation and ideas.

C uisine Actuelle is a new cookbook which totally and appropriately reflects the food philosophy of Victor Gielisse as well as that of his renowned restaurant, Actuelle, in Dallas. As one of only forty-four Certified Master Chefs in the United States, Victor Gielisse can draw on an impressive professional background and many unique experiences as he brings to the reader a wealth of information and a series of highly interesting and reliable recipes.

Not only does this book span everything from appetizers to desserts, starting with Parma-wrapped Prawns and ending with a Potted Ginger Cream, but, more importantly, it features recipes which are *inspirations* for those who seek to add more unique dishes to their repertoire.

Cuisine Actuelle offers fresh, interesting approaches, many of which draw on Victor's experience as a member of the World-Cup-winning U.S. Culinary team in Luxembourg, his experience as a Certified Master Chef, and his very successful participation in many national recipe contests, in which he frequently gathered the top prize. It can serve as an enjoyable guide to creative cooking.

Indeed, *Cuisine Actuelle* should become a part of every amateur cook's library; however, it can also serve as an invaluable resource for the professional chef who is not threatened by creative approaches to and new ideas about food.

FERDINAND E. METZ, C.M.C.

INTRODUCTION

One can never know too much; the more one learns, the more one sees the need to learn more and that study, as well as broadening the mind of the craftsman, provides an easy way of perfecting yourself in the practice of your art.

AUGUSTE ESCOFFIER

I n this age of fast lifestyles and high technology we often forget or take for granted the simplest of pleasures. . . .

I grew up in Holland, where the dinner table was the social gathering point of the day. Our family's time together there was the highlight of our day. Although those years passed quickly, I often think back to our discussions of the day's activities as we enjoyed our meal. My mother was a fabulous cook and instilled in me my appreciation and passion for food. Born into a family of restaurateurs and hoteliers, I saw up close the demanding work schedule my father put in day after day, year in year out. But there is something mystical and exciting about our trade—not one day is the same. Cooking is not just my profession, it is my hobby, my life. Everything I do revolves around cooking.

Hippocrates once said, "The life so short, the craft so long to learn," and this certainly applies to the culinary trade— nothing takes the place of experience.

Cooking is fun, relaxing, and exciting. It is both art and culture. And if you use the solid principles of cooking as a foundation, your creativity will flourish and your individual style will develop.

As a chef, I feel blessed with bringing added enjoyment to the meal. In the restaurant, after a night's service, nothing is more gratifying than hearing a guest say, "Thank you, it was a wonderful meal!" This is the recognition, the culmination of a day's work, that makes it all worthwhile.

This book combines recipes from our restaurant, Actuelle, with wisdom gained from my years in this profession and the wonderful experiences and ideas I was able to share with talented fellow chefs throughout the world. There are no secret ingredients in my cooking because, quite simply, in cooking there are no secrets. Certainly, throughout the years chefs have taught me techniques to enhance flavor and techniques to perfect a specific cooking method, but all these are learned. I firmly believe that success is based on one's ability to accept a continuous learning experience. *Cuisine Actuelle* demonstrates a wide variety of foods and techniques. Despite this era of innovation in cooking and the convergence of cuisines from around the globe, the essentials of sound and proven culinary principles must apply. Regardless of origin or ethnic background, the dishes represented in this cookbook reflect this philosophy and depend on choice ingredients for their success.

I hope you have fun while you explore the recipes in this book, and remember, happy people means happy cooking!

VICTOR A. L. GIELISSE, C.M.C.

Seasoning

Contrary to popular belief, seasoning need not follow strict guidelines. Many cookbooks do not even specify quantities for seasonings. Often, established culinary terms are used rather than precise measurements. Some examples are: *aromatiser* (to add aroma); *exicer* (to add spice or herbs); and *assaisoner* (bring to taste). The use of fresh herbs is still under-utilized in today's kitchens.

Use fresh herbs when possible, as the natural juices and aroma are preserved. Certain herbs are best when added at the last moment to ensure optimum flavor. Some of these more delicate herbs are: chives, parsley, dill, chervil, lemon-grass, and tarragon. Herbs which can tolerate the cooking process include: oregano, thyme, marjoram, cilantro, fennel, and peppermint.

When purchasing spices, buy small quantities and store in air-tight containers in a cool, dry place. Shelf life is six months, to ensure an adequate amount of aroma.

You can use many other items in the kitchen to season a dish: vinegars and citrus fruits add tartness; shallots, garlic, and chives add a more intense flavor (bitterness); sugars, honey, and fruit syrups add sweetness.

Through the centuries, the value of herbs and spices in both the medical and culinary fields has been proven. Herbs and spices can actually increase the appetite and promote proper digestion. It is also interesting to note that herbs and spices contain substantial vitamins, oils, and minerals, and act as natural preservatives to deter spoilage of food.

Despite the increased awareness of a healthful cuisine which limits the use of salt, salt is still a very important mineral and seasoning agent. There are very few dishes in the culinary repertoire that do not require the addition of some salt; however, moderation is the key factor from both a medical and a culinary perspective. Fresh herbs play a particularly important role in seasoning sodium- or fat-free diets as a salt-substitute.

Today's chef must exercise the principles of cooking based on the solid fundamentals and influenced by the four basic taste sensations: salty, sour, sweet, and bitter. Be creative with flavors that not only excite and stimulate the palate, but also make sense.

Above all, remember that everything created must provide the proper balance of nutrition, texture, and taste. Seasoning does not just happen, it is inspired by the chef's individuality, style, experience, and taste.

Fish and Shellfish

Fish and shellfish are appearing more frequently on menus, both in restaurants and at home. Per capita consumption has grown steadily each year. Yes, we are changing our eating habits—but today's average American diet still contains too much fat. For better balanced nutrition and health, fat intake must be reduced. Seafood is an excellent solution.

The increased popularity of seafood can be attributed to its nutritional value. It is an excellent source of protein, minerals, and vitamins. The rising demand for fish and shellfish has contributed to an increased availability of a variety of seafoods on today's market. This availability, combined with versatility of preparation, leads to an exciting array of recipe possibilities.

The challenge for today's chef is to make cooking better without complicating it, and his most important goal is to arrive at a nutritionally balanced dish that is both flavorful and appealing to the eye. Armed with sound knowledge and using simple methods of preparation and presentation, this goal becomes a continuing—and exciting—experiment.

FAT CONTENT AND METHODS OF PREPARATION

Finfish and shellfish are divided into groups based on similarity of taste, texture, color of meat, and richness. Fish with a low fat content are white or light in color. They are mild in flavor and tend to be tender and flaky when cooked. Some examples of fish with a low fat content (up to 2.5%) are: sole, flounder, snapper, grouper, cod, Pacific halibut, haddock, and sea bass. Poaching, steaming, and other moist heat techniques are most suitable for these delicate fish and will prevent the fish from drying out. If baking, broiling, sautéing or grilling these types of fish, take extreme caution to avoid loss of moisture. Fish with a higher fat content are darker, richer in flavor, and more suited to dry heat techniques; examples include: tuna, sturgeon, swordfish, and mahi-mahi.

SHELLFISH

Shellfish are divided into two groups: crustaceans and mollusks. Crustaceans include: lobster, crab, shrimp, crayfish, and spiny lobster. Mollusks are double-shelled species such as: oysters, clams, mussels, or without shells: squid and octopus. Crustaceans are most frequently steamed or poached, whereas mollusks lend themselves to steaming and sautéing.

PURCHASING FISH

Purchasing fish is a challenge on its own. Buy only the freshest and highest quality seafood. Establish a trusting relationship with your supplier. The store where you purchase your seafood should look and smell clean. Fish does have an odor, but it should be a mild, sweet, sea-like smell. Fish should be displayed properly on plenty of ice.

Most fish, when purchased, are already eviscerated, gutted, and scaled, and the gills removed. If scales are on the fish make sure they are firmly attached to the skin and have a bright shine. After removing scales the skin will appear very moist. Look for well-rounded, bright, clear and protruding eyes. Gills are real age indicators; they should be pink-red or red, never green or brown. Flesh must feel firm to the touch. Should the fish have been improperly handled there will be an imprint left in the flesh.

PERFECTLY COOKED

How does one know when fish is perfectly cooked? It should not be transparent and should just flake when touched with a fork; shellfish becomes firm and opaque.

Whichever cooking method one chooses is really not the most important factor. What is crucial is not to overcook seafood. Freshness, too, is of the essence. Seafood will lose most of its flavor, in addition to becoming tough and rubbery, when it is not fresh.

AQUA-CULTURE

Aqua-culture is by no means new—it has existed for some 3000 years. The Orient has already experimented with fish raised in controlled conditions. Most of today's trout, catfish, crawfish, and oysters are pond-raised or cultured. Other species in major production now are fresh-water prawns, carp, baby coho salmon, and blackfish. Research and study are well under way on the aqua-culture of lobster, bass, clams, and abalone. Pond-raised or aqua-culture will play an important role in the future of the seafood industry.

CATFISH

Catfish has tremendous possibilities for the future. Pond-raised by the millions of pounds annually, a rapidly growing demand is making this fish "chic." Traditionally thought of as a poor man's fish and a mud scavenger, catfish have won over new fans: more and more Americans are trying the pond-raised product. Catfish are firm and mild, and their moist fresh-water flavor makes them virtually odorless. Catfish are excellent for frying, sautéing, braising, and steaming. The catfish has adapted well to aqua-culture as long as pond waters are clean and well-oxygenated. Ninety-five percent of the farm-raised catfish are from Mississippi. Other states include Alabama, Louisiana, and Texas. Yearly over 400 million pounds are processed, which is eight and one-half percent plus or minus of the total fish and seafood market in the United States. We can see why this fish of the South is looking for the respect it so rightfully deserves.

RED SNAPPER

Red Snapper is one of the most delicious deep-sea delicacies on today's market and is available in many varieties. Caught in the Gulf of Mexico and landed in Florida, where most of the red snapper industry is centered, it is available year-round in all parts of the country. With its juicy white meat and delicate flavor, red snapper is suitable for a variety of cooking applications. Little is actually known of this fish that ranges up to 30 pounds and 2½ feet in length. A great fish for sautéing and or any moist-heat cooking method.

OYSTERS

Oysters have been enjoyed for many centuries. In fact, oyster farming has been practiced in the West since the days of the Romans, and oysters were cultivated in the Far East long before the Christian era. American coastlines are blessed with public oyster beds, yet most of today's market is farm-raised along the coastal shorelines of many states. The most common oyster, the Eastern, or Atlantic, is found from the Gulf Coast to Cape Cod. The Eastern oyster represents 85% of the total production. Two other species of commercial value are the Pacific and the rare Western or Olympia oyster. Oysters are an excellent source of protein, minerals, and vitamins and are easily digested. Never overcook oysters as they need to remain plump and tender. Oysters can be cooked by a variety of methods, fried, sautéed, poached, braised, baked or served raw. ***Purchase oysters only from reputable stores.***

SHRIMP

Shrimp are the most popular shellfish in the United States. A ten-legged crustacean, its name is derived from the middle English word *shrimpe* meaning puny person, or the Swedish word *skrympa* meaning to shrink. There are three main varieties: the northern, the north Pacific, and the southern. The southern shrimp is taken from the Gulf and south Atlantic states. Southern shrimp are the largest species. Commercially available southern shrimp is white, brown, and pink or brown-spotted. Shrimp are excellent sources of high-quality protein, minerals, vitamins, and are low in both fat and calories. The cooked product is tender, delicate, and delicious.

Even today it appears that too many people are still uneasy about fish preparation. A reintroduction of the product and what to do with it is necessary, especially now that the market is flooded with under-utilized seafood products such as skate, shark, roughy, buffalo fish, tile fish, squid, porgy, angelfish, etc.

Fresh fish tastes best if it is handled as little as possible. Let its natural flavor and texture come through. Enhance a dish with lighter sauces. Balance seasonings and utilize fresh vegetable purées and fruit vinegars. A reduced fish stock with ginger and citrus fruits on top of simple steamed bass seasoned with bay leaf and peppercorns will delight diners.

In my cuisine, I attempt to strike the proper balance between the different regional influences: Oriental; the ever popular Mexican flavor of the Southwest; the Midwest with trends of Scandinavia and Germany; the German-Dutch influence in Pennsylvania; and New England's cuisine, with its deep roots dating back to the Anglo-Saxons. The variety of ethnic groups, each with their own culinary background, brings tremendous excitement to cuisine in America.

There has been a refreshing change in attitude towards cooking in America. American cuisine is becoming recognized throughout the world and a tremendous leap is being made towards the research and development of the cuisine of tomorrow.

In essence, all cuisine is based on solid cooking principles. From there we interpret, adjust, search, develop, and accommodate. Creativity and innovation are the challenge for chefs today.

A Word on Wine

"A word on wine," was the directive. Victor asked me to include a few words on wine to accompany his opus. A glass of wine to complement a meal; strings with a symphony; the two go hand in hand.

My enjoyment of wine developed from my upbringing in a family which certainly knows how to enjoy the best in food and wine. My mother is an excellent cook and we travelled extensively, sampling the cuisines and wines of the world. This is coupled with my years in the hospitality business and my responsibility for the wine list at Actuelle.

If you want to learn about wine, there are a number of great authorities on the subject: Michael Broadbent, Hugh Johnson, Alexis Lichine, Robert M. Parker, Jr., and Frank Schoonmaker, to name a few. Kevin Zraly's *Windows on the World Complete Wine Course* makes an excellent introduction for the wine student. Or, subscribe to one or more of the wine periodicals, such as: *Connoisseur's Guide, The Wine Advocate,* or *The Wine Spectator.* Watch for "Best Buys" in the supermarket or wine shop. These make an excellent way to experiment inexpensively as you find your way through the complexities of wine. Start with the varietals: Chardonnay, Sauvignon Blanc, Cabernet Sauvignon, Pinot Noir, etc. You will learn the characteristics of each grape variety and be able to apply this experience as you learn about the great wines of Bordeaux, Burgundy, and the other wine regions of the world.

Most important: drink what you like. If you enjoy red wine with fish, that's alright; white wine need not always accompany white meat. A softer red wine, such as a Pinot Noir, can be a perfect accompaniment to a richer fish like salmon. Sweeter wines should not be neglected. An off-dry Riesling or a Gewurztraminer make a nice aperitif or an excellent foil to spicier foods. A very sweet wine, such as a Sauterne, is an unbeatable match with desserts or a pungent cheese like Stilton. Why not forget the cocktail and start with an aperitif? A glass of Sauvignon Blanc, a dry Sherry, Dubonnet, Lillet, or a glass of Champagne, for instance, will enhance the appetite and make the perfect start to a meal. On Champagne, drink it anytime, before, during or after a meal— don't wait for a special occasion.

But most of all, *enjoy* wine. Do not be intimidated by wine or the opinions of those who would attempt to restrict your safe and responsible enjoyment of this delightful beverage. Moderate drinking has been proven to reduce stress, aid digestion, and lead to a longer, more satisfying life.

Cheers.

CLIVE O'DONOGHUE

MENUS FOR ALL SEASONS

SPRING

*Sweetwater Prawns with Parma in Phyllo
and Papaya-Tomato Relish*

Roma Tomato Basil Soup

*Pan-seared Duck Breast with Red Currant Sauce
Spaetzle and Asparagus*

Crème Brûlee in Spiced Cookie Shell

BYRON 1989 RESERVE CHARDONNAY

Potato and Celery Strudel with Burnet and Arugula Greens

Three Pepper Gazpacho Soup with Speckled Cornbread Muffins

Pan-seared Snapper on Curried Roasted Vegetables

Poached Pinot Noir Pears with Butterscotch Sauce

J. LOHR 1990 CHARDONNAY RIVERSTONE

SUMMER

*Tartare of Salmon, Tomato Mayonnaise, and Cilantro Dressing on
Toast Points*

Smoked Chicken and Three Pepper Soup with Baby Corn

*Three-nut-crusted Pork Tenderloin with
Green Apple Tomatillo Relish*

Chocolate Praline Raisin Bread Pudding

BOUCHAINE CARNEROS CHARDONNAY 1988

Grilled Pork Saté with Peanut Sauce

Confit of Duck with Young Green Beans and Walnut Vinaigrette

Red Snapper Dumplings with Jicama and Mushrooms
Lemon Thyme Potato Pie

Lemon-Lime Tart with Raspberry Sauce

LES VIEUX CEPAGES 1990 GRENACHE ROSE

FALL

Mountain Grass and Heather Honey Salmon
Tarragon Mayonnaise and Savory Potato Pancake

Chilled Pumpkin and Apple Soup

Braised Lamb Shank with Parsnips, Carrots, and Risotto

Tequila-Lime and Pink Grapefruit Sorbets
with Almond Hazelnut Stick Cookies

CHATEAU THIELEY BORDEAUX 1989

Scallops in Fennel and Basil Vinaigrette with Mixed Greens

Corn Chowder with Leeks and Bell Peppers

Gingered Chicken Ragout with Linguine and Bean Sprouts

Pineapple Beignets with Southern Comfort Eggnog

CLOS DU BOIS WINEMAKER RESERVE 1988
RUSSIAN RIVER VALLEY CHARDONNAY

WINTER

Spicy Pork Pockets with Papaya, Corn, and Red Pepper Relish

Minted Fish and Shellfish Soup with Celeriac

Grilled Lambloin Chop with Peppered Pineapple

Spinach Mousse

Plum, Pear and Apple Compote in Phyllo with Mascarpone Amaretto Creme

WILLIAM WHEELER 1988 RS RESERVE
CALIFORNIA RED TABLE WINE

Blue Crab, Oyster and Prawn Sausage with Deviled Corn and Tomato Salsa

Parsnip and Carrot Soup with Tarragon

Grilled Pork Loin in Apricot and Curry Marinade Tomato Risotto

Maple Apples

Bailey's Chocolate Ricotta Mousse Cake with Bailey's Creme Anglaise

MERRY VALE VINEYARDS 1989 STARMONT

A SPECIAL MENU

HEALTHFUL CUISINE FOR CONTEMPORARY LIVING

America is in the midst of a gigantic shift in public attitude toward improving the quality of life and health. Recent surveys confirm that 60% of the nation's adults are making changes in at-home eating habits to comply with the recommended dietary guidelines. Proof enough that the population now takes the old proverb, "you are what you eat," seriously.

This new American epicureanism has spawned a revival of home cooking that is unparalleled in the history of culinary arts. That's why this section of *Cuisine Actuelle* has been written. Designed to meet the current demand for a lighter, more nutritious way of dining, the following menu provides healthful and imaginative recipes well-suited for today's active lifestyle.

Why leaner cuisine? USDA studies of food intake show the whole nation cutting down on fat and moving toward nutritional goals the public understands. Victor Gielisse reflects this commitment to wellness by combining fresh, wholesome ingredients at the peak of their season and showcasing them in attractive and flavorful menus at Actuelle. He is also more than accommodating when it comes to providing healthy options for Actuelle's loyal clientele. Actuelle's fare includes a wide variety of non-cream-based sauces such as vegetable purées, citrus and fruit vinegar blends. And as one of the first culinarians to support a liaison between chefs and nutrition professionals, Victor adapts this menu from existing recipes in the Actuelle repertoire, answering the need for:

- **Simple Preparation Methods**
  To save time and enhance natural flavors;

- **Nutritionally Balanced Menus**
  With ingredients selected to complement one another in color, taste and texture;

- **Attention to the Dietary Guidelines for Good Health**

- **Helpful Hints**

  Offering preparation tips and serving suggestions for each recipe; and

• **A Shopping Guide**
　　With a master ingredient list for each menu to minimize effort in executing the meal plan.

In summary, the recipes which follow demonstrate that America doesn't have to give up the thrill of preparing a culinary work of art in favor of nutritional value. Taking the reader through a full menu of flavor, this chapter is destined to become the working tool of the novice cook who longs to create something delightful to taste without shortchanging a healthy future.

Nancy Skodack, M.S., R.D./L.D.

MENU

Appetizer
Pan-Seared Duck with Ginger and Cilantro
with Orzo and Jicama Salad

Soup
Vegetable Beef and Barley Soup

Main Course
Catfish Fillets with Apple-Tomatillo Sauce and
Sweet Bell Peppers

Dessert
Fresh Fruit with Cactus Pear and Mango Sauce

This menu has been analyzed by computer and found to be in compliance with the Recommended Dietary Guidelines for All Healthy Americans with 30% of total calories from fat, 20% from protein, and 50% from carbohydrates.

SHOPPING GUIDE

MEAT AND FISH

4 3-ounce	Raw duck breasts
6 ounce	Raw flank steak
12 ounces	Raw catfish fillets

PRODUCE

1	Gingerroot
1	Bulb garlic
1	White onion
1	Turnip
1	Bulb celeriac
1	Medium jicama
1	Cucumber
1	Red bell pepper
1	Yellow bell pepper
1	Green bell pepper
1	Serrano pepper
⅓ pound	Green asparagus
2	Carrots
1	Stalk celery
4	Red oak leaves
1	Bunch shallots
1	Leek
⅔ pound	Shiitake mushrooms
1	Bunch chives
1	Bunch basil
1	Bunch cilantro
1	Bunch mint
1	Bunch edible flowers
½ pound	Tomatillos
1	Roma tomato
4	Cactus pears
3	Golden Delicious apples
1	Half-pint raspberries
1	Half-pint blueberries
2	Mangoes
2	Oranges
1	Grapefruit
½	Medium cantaloupe
½	Medium pineapple

CONDIMENTS AND GROCERIES

1	Package orzo pasta
1	Package barley pearls
⅓ cup	Rice wine vinegar
1 tablespoon	Raspberry vinegar
2 tablespoons	Corn oil
1½ tablespoons	Canola oil
1 tablespoon	Olive oil

STAPLES

Cracked pepper and salt

PAN-SEARED DUCK WITH GINGER AND
CILANTRO WITH ORZO AND JICAMA SALAD

Serves 4

Preheat oven to 350°. Marinate duck breasts in 1 tablespoon of the canola oil, gingerroot, garlic, basil, cilantro, and white pepper for 1 hour.

In mixing bowl combine the cucumber, jicama, bell pepper, tomato, and orzo. Add chicken stock. Season with rice wine vinegar and pepper. Add the remaining ½ tablespoon canola oil. Combine well and chill for 1 hour. Heat large skillet until very hot. Pan-sear the duck breasts in skillet. Quickly brown both sides. Remove from heat and finish cooking in preheated 350° oven for 3 minutes. Allow cooked duck breasts to rest for 2 minutes; then slice fan-tail style and serve with jicama salad. Garnish each portion with a sprig of chives, red oak leaf, and edible flower.

4 3-ounce	Duck breasts, skinned and visible fat removed
1½ tablespoons	Canola oil
1 teaspoon	Grated gingerroot
½ teaspoon	Minced garlic
½ tablespoon	Chopped basil
½ tablespoon	Chopped cilantro
½ teaspoon	Fresh cracked white pepper
1 medium	Cucumber, cleaned and finely diced
1 medium	Jicama, cleaned and finely diced
1	Red bell pepper, cleaned, seeded, and diced
1	Roma tomato, peeled, seeded, and diced
2 cups	Cooked orzo (rice-shaped pasta)
2 tablespoons	Chicken stock
⅓ cup	Rice wine vinegar
½ teaspoon	Fresh cracked pepper
	Sprig of fresh chives
4	Red oak leaves
	Edible flowers (such as pansies or nasturtiums)

VEGETABLE BEEF AND BARLEY SOUP

Serves 6

1 tablespoon	Olive oil
⅓ cup	Diced carrots
⅓ cup	Diced celery
⅓ cup	Diced onions
⅓ cup	Diced turnips
⅓ cup	Diced celeriac
1½ quart	Clear vegetable stock or chicken stock
⅓ cup	Cooked pearl barley
1 cup	Shiitake mushrooms, diced
4 ounces	Cooked flank steak, parboiled and diced
1 tablespoon	Chopped cilantro
½ teaspoon	Cracked pepper

In medium stockpot, heat oil. Add carrots, celery, onions, turnips, and celeriac. Sweat for 5 minutes over medium heat until translucent and glossy. Add clear vegetable stock. Bring to a rapid boil. Add barley. Simmer for 20 minutes. Add shiitake mushrooms and flank steak. Simmer an additional 20 minutes. Season with cilantro and pepper.

CATFISH FILLETS WITH APPLE-TOMATILLO SAUCE AND SWEET BELL PEPPERS

Serves 4

Sauce Preparation

⅓ cup	Leeks, diced
3	Golden Delicious apples, peeled, seeded, and diced
1	Serrano pepper, seeded and minced
2 tablespoons	Corn oil
2 teaspoons	Garlic, minced
3 teaspoons	Shallots, finely chopped
1 cup	Chicken stock
½ pound	Tomatillos, husks removed and diced

In a medium saucepan combine leeks, apples, serrano pepper, 1 tablespoon and 2 teaspoons of the corn oil, 1 teaspoon of the garlic, and 2 teaspoons of the shallots. Cook and stir over low heat for 6 minutes.

Stir in chicken stock and tomatillos. Bring to a rapid boil, stirring constantly; then reduce heat and simmer, stirring occasionally, for 20 minutes. Cool the tomatillo mixture slightly.

Pour the cooled mixture into the jar of an electric blender. Cover and blend until the mixture is of uniform consistency. Using a coarse sieve, strain the tomatillo mixture into a saucepan, forcing as much of the pulp through the strainer as possible. Set aside.

Catfish Preparation

Preheat the oven to 350°. Brush a large sauté pan with the remaining teaspoon of corn oil. Sprinkle with the remaining garlic and shallots.

Place catfish fillets into the prepared pan. Add the fish stock. Cover with a large piece of parchment paper. Bake in preheated oven for 6 minutes.

While fish is cooking, slice the red, yellow, and green bell peppers into julienne strips. Wash and trim the asparagus tips. In a saucepan combine the peppers and asparagus with a small amount of slightly salted water. Bring to boiling; reduce heat and simmer for 2 minutes over low heat.

Just before serving, add the cilantro, cracked pepper, and salt to the strained tomatillo mixture. Strain the cooking liquid from the catfish; add to tomatillo mixture. Heat through.

To serve, place equal portions of the pepper mixture on top half of 4 heated dinner plates. Display 3 cooked catfish fillets on the lower half of each plate with 1 tablespoon of the tomatillo sauce carefully ladled between each fillet. Garnish with minced red pepper. Finish off the plate presentation with a leaf of fresh basil.

12 ounces	Mississippi farm-raised catfish fillets, cut into 12 portions
⅓ cup	Fish stock
	Parchment paper
½ each	Red, yellow, and green bell peppers
9 stalks	Tender green asparagus
3 tablespoons	Chopped fresh cilantro
1 teaspoon	Fresh cracked pepper
⅛ teaspoon	Salt
	Minced red pepper
4 leaves	Fresh basil

FRESH FRUIT WITH CACTUS PEAR AND MANGO SAUCE

Sauce

1	**Mango, pitted and peeled**
4	**Cactus pears, pitted, seeded and passed through a sieve**
	Juice of 1 fresh orange
1 tablespoon	**Raspberry vinegar**
½ teaspoon	**Cracked white pepper**

Fruit

1	**Grapefruit, peeled, seeded, and cut into 12 sections**
1	**Mango, peeled, seeded, and cut into 12 sections**
½ medium	**Cantaloupe, peeled, seeded, and sliced into 12 sections**
½ medium	**Pineapple, peeled, cored, and sliced lengthwise into 12 julienne strips**

Garnish

1 pint	**Red raspberries**
½ pint	**Fresh blueberries**
	Fresh mint leaves

To prepare sauce, cut mango into chunks. In a food processor combine mangos, sieved cactus pears, fresh orange juice, raspberry vinegar, and pepper. Blend in food processor. Chill.

To dress dessert plate, place equal portions of the mango sauce on 4 plates. Artfully arrange sliced fresh fruits over sauce. Garnish with raspberries, blueberries, and fresh mint.

APPETIZERS

FRESH SNAIL MOUSSELINE

Serves 6 (12 darioles)

60	Fresh "Petite Gris" snails (farm-raised in California), no shell
¼ pound	Butter
1 tablespoon	Olive oil
8 cloves	Shallots, finely chopped
8 cloves	Garlic, finely minced
⅓ cup	Good quality Brandy
⅓ cup	Good quality red wine
⅓ cup	Chicken stock
1 pound	Shiitake mushrooms, cleaned, stalks removed, and diced
3 tablespoons	Finely snipped fresh basil
3 tablespoons	Finely snipped fresh chives
1 tablespoon	Finely snipped fresh tarragon
1 tablespoon	Finely snipped fresh cilantro
	Freshly ground pepper
	Salt
1 pound	Chicken breast, boneless, fat-free, skinless
3	Egg whites
1 cup	Heavy cream
	Clarified butter
30 sheets	Phyllo dough

Blanch snails in vinegar water; stir and drain. In a large sauté pan melt butter and add olive oil. Add shallots and garlic; sweat briefly until glossy. Add snails and cook over low heat for 2 minutes. Add brandy, red wine, and chicken stock; simmer. Add mushrooms and simmer over low heat for 30 minutes, stirring frequently. Add basil, chives and tarragon. Add cilantro and season with pepper. Simmer for 5 additional minutes until almost all liquid has reduced. Adjust salt and pepper. Pour mixture onto a baking sheet and cool.

Prepare a chicken forcemeat from chicken, egg white, and cream. Keep cool in bowl over ice. Fold chicken mousse into the snail-mushroom mixture. Test small amount and taste. Adjust seasoning. Brush dariole molds or ramekins with clarified butter. Divide mixture evenly making sure there are five snails in each ramekin. Place ramekins in an insert pan with a little hot water and bake in 375° oven for 25 minutes or until firm to the touch. Do not overcook. Remove from oven and let rest for 5 minutes before removing from molds. Cool thoroughly.

Brush phyllo dough with clarified butter. Cut phyllo dough in half. Wrap snail mousselines in dough using 4 half-sheets per mousseline. Brush tops with clarified butter.

When ready to serve, bake in 375° oven for 10 minutes or until evenly browned. Serve at once.

SWEETWATER PRAWNS WITH PARMA IN PHYLLO

Serves 6

Parma ham (seasoned, salt-cured, and air-dried—not smoked) comes from the best swine farms in the Lombardia, Piemonte, and Emilia Romagna regions of Italy, as well as Veneto, the village of Lang Lirano, south of the city of Parma. The taste is unmatched and the aroma is of such quality that there is frankly no comparison to domestic prosciutto. You will find Parma ham in fine grocery stores. It is sometimes called true prosciutto.

In large mixing bowl combine oil, gingerroot, garlic, rosemary, thyme, vodka, and pepper. Add prawns; toss to coat. Cover and refrigerate for 3 hours.

Remove prawns from marinade and wrap each in ham. Butter and layer 3 sheets of phyllo dough. Cut phyllo dough widthwise into 1 inch wide strips. Wrap phyllo dough around prawns to form natural shape of prawn. Brush outside with butter and refrigerate for 1 hour. Repeat procedure until all prawns are wrapped.

Place phyllo-wrapped prawns on cookie sheet and bake in preheated 400° oven for 8 to 12 minutes or until golden brown.

Serve hot with Papaya-Tomato Relish.

5 tablespoons	Olive oil
2 tablespoons	Fresh minced gingerroot
2 cloves	Garlic, minced
2 teaspoons	Fresh minced rosemary
2 teaspoons	Minced lemon thyme
5 tablespoons	Vodka
½ teaspoon	Ground black pepper
24 jumbo	Sweetwater prawns or jumbo shrimp, peeled and deveined
12 thin slices	Parma ham, cut in half lengthwise
12 sheets	Phyllo dough
2¼ cups	Clarified butter Papaya-Tomato Relish (*p. 65*)

SHRIMP WITH LEEKS AND ENDIVE

Serves 4

1 pound	Shrimp (10 to 15 per pound)
2 tablespoons	Brandy
3 tablespoons	White wine
3 whole	Roma tomatoes, seeded and diced
½ cup	Heavy cream
1 clove	Shallot, minced
2 cloves	Garlic, minced
1 sprig	Lemon thyme
2	Leeks, diced
1	Belgian endive, diced
3 tablespoons	Butter
⅔ cup	Fish stock or vegetable stock
	Salt
	Pepper
	Ground nutmeg

Shell the shrimp and reserve and chop the shells. Sauté the shells in a very hot skillet for 2 minutes; flame with brandy and add white wine. Add tomato, cream, shallot, garlic, and thyme. Simmer for 2 minutes. Pass through large kitchen sieve, crushing shells to get maximum flavor. Season with a little salt and pepper and set aside. Keep warm.

Sauté leek and endive in butter. Add stock and simmer slowly until tender. Adjust seasoning with salt, pepper, and nutmeg. Sauté shrimp quickly in hot skillet and brown evenly.

Place leek and endive mixture in a casserole; top with shrimp. Keep warm. Pour tomato mixture on top.

SCALLOPS IN FENNEL AND BASIL VINAIGRETTE

Serves 6

In a medium saucepan cook onion, celery, and garlic in hot oil until tender. Add stock, wine, lime juice, and fennel. Add basil, bay leaf, and peppercorns and simmer for 15 minutes. In a shallow dish place sliced scallops. Pour hot fennel mixture on top and let sit for 15 minutes. Toss scallops gently with dressing and adjust with salt and pepper. Divide scallops into even portions and serve with mixed greens.

1 pound	Sea scallops, cleaned, muscle removed, and cut in half (10 to 20 per pound)
1 medium	Red onion, finely diced
1 stalk	Celery, finely diced
2 cloves	Garlic, minced
4 tablespoons	Virgin olive oil
1½ cups	Fish stock
½ cup	White wine
¼ cup	Lime juice
1 teaspoon	Cracked fennel seeds
2 tablespoons	Snipped basil
1	Bay leaf
8	White peppercorns, cracked
	Salt
	Pepper
	Mixed greens such as radicchio, endive, escarole, and arugula

MOUNTAIN GRASS AND HEATHER HONEY SALMON

Makes 25 portions

1 side	Norwegian salmon, deboned and cleaned with skin intact (3 to 4 pounds total)
2 tablespoons	Brown sugar
2 tablespoons	Salt
1 bunch	Dill, snipped
4 tablespoons	Mixed peppercorns, crushed
2 tablespoons	Lemon thyme leaves
6 tablespoons	Okhotnichya vodka

Rinse salmon; pat dry with a paper towel: Place salmon in a large stainless steel pan, skin side down. Rub salmon with sugar and salt. Add the dill, peppercorns, and thyme. Drizzle with the vodka. Cover with plastic wrap and place in refrigerator. Marinate for 24 hours. Remove from refrigerator and repeat procedure by placing salmon in clean pan and sprinkling a little salt on the bottom of the pan. This will help prevent any juices secreted from the salmon from turning sour. Cover with fresh wrap and return to refrigerator to marinate for an additional 12 hours. Slice salmon thinly and serve with tarragon mayonnaise and Savory Potato Pancakes (*page 110*). Serve salmon well chilled.

TARTARE OF SALMON

Serves 8

Combine salmon, onions, capers, and chives. Fold in yolks, lemon juice, and olive oil. Season with cilantro, rice wine vinegar, Worcestershire sauce, salt, and pepper. Serve on toast points.

1 pound	**Center-cut salmon, cleaned, de-boned, and chopped**
4 tablespoons	**Finely chopped onion**
4 tablespoons	**Finely chopped capers**
2 tablespoons	**Finely chopped chives**
2	**Egg yolks**
2 tablespoons	**Lemon juice**
1 tablespoon	**Olive oil**
1 tablespoon	**Finely chopped cilantro**
½ teaspoon	**Rice wine vinegar**
½ teaspoon	**Worcestershire sauce**
	Salt
	Fresh pepper
	Toast points

POTATO, CRABMEAT, AND CHEESE STRUDEL

Makes 2 strudels; serves 12

1 pound	Potatoes, peeled
½ pound	Lump crabmeat, cleaned
1	Medium red onion, diced
3 cloves	Minced garlic
⅓ cup	Canola oil
⅓ cup	Chicken stock
½ pound	Button mushrooms, cleaned and sliced
2	Large Porcini or Cepe mushrooms, diced
4 tablespoons	Brandy
2 tablespoons	Snipped basil
2 tablespoons	Snipped cilantro
1 tablespoon	Snipped lemon thyme
	Freshly cracked pepper
	Salt
½ cup	Grated Gruyère cheese
3	Egg yolks
8 sheets	Phyllo dough
	Clarified butter

Slice potato thinly; blanch in salted water and drain. Spread on a cookie sheet to cool quickly.

In sauté pan cook crabmeat, red onion, and garlic in half of the oil. Add chicken stock, button mushrooms, porcini mushrooms, and brandy. Simmer slowly for 3 minutes; set aside. In sauté pan heat remaining oil and sauté the cooled potato slices until golden brown. Season with basil, cilantro, thyme, pepper, and salt. Combine with crab and mushroom mixture. Heat thoroughly. Cool.

In a mixing bowl mix Gruyère with egg yolks. Fold into cooled crab and mushroom mixture.

On a clean surface, spread phyllo sheets. Place 4 sheets on top of each other, brushing each with butter except the top one. Spread evenly with half of the crab mixture, then roll into a cylindrical shape. Brush with butter and place on a cookie sheet. Repeat with remaining mixture and phyllo dough. Rest 1 hour in refrigerator.

Bake in 375° oven about 6 minutes or until golden brown on all sides. Cool slightly and slice. Serve with a tossed salad.

BLUE CRAB, OYSTER, AND PRAWN SAUSAGE

Serves 8

Place prawns in a bowl over ice. Chill food processor bowl and blade. The key here depends on all ingredients being of an even temperature: *Cold.* Purée half of the prawns in chilled food processor at pulse speed for 30 seconds. Stop and clean sides. Use pulse speed again for 30 seconds. Add unbeaten egg whites and run at regular speed for 45 seconds. Add half of the cream and run for 30 seconds more. Remove from food processor. Put mixture in a bowl and place bowl over ice. Fold in the remaining cream. Fold in remaining prawns, crabmeat and oysters. Season with dill, basil, tarragon, salt, and pepper. Adjust seasonings, if necessary. Pipe mixture into casings with pastry bag using a large round nozzle. Tie casings at 4 inch intervals. Poach sausages in court bouillon or stock for 3 minutes. Place sausages in ice bath. Reheat and serve in seasoned stock.

½ pound	Gulf prawns, cleaned and diced
2	Egg whites
1 cup	Heavy cream
8 ounces	Prawns (clean, cook, dice)
8 ounces	Blue crab meat (clean, cook)
8 ounces	Oysters (shuck, clean cook, dice)
2 tablespoons	Dill
2 tablespoons	Basil
2 tablespoons	Tarragon
1 teaspoon	Salt
½ teaspoon	White pepper
1 quart	Court bouillon or fish stock

POTATO AND CELERY STRUDEL WITH BURNET AND ARUGULA GREENS

Serves 8

1 pound	Celery root, cleaned and peeled
½ pound	Potatoes, cleaned and peeled
4 tablespoons	Olive oil
½ pound	Shiitake mushrooms, stems removed and sliced
2 cloves	Garlic, minced
2 cloves	Shallots, minced
2 tablespoons	Finely snipped basil
2 tablespoons	Snipped cilantro
	Salt and freshly cracked pepper
¼ cup	Grated Asiago cheese
4	Egg yolks
6 sheets	Phyllo dough (spread out on work area and kept covered with plastic wrap)
	Clarified butter
	Arugula and burnet leaves, tossed in vinaigrette

Slice celery root and potato into thin slices. Blanch in salted water or stock; drain. Spread on a plate or tray to cool quickly. Heat oil in sauté pan and add mushrooms, garlic, and shallots. Cook over low heat for 1 minute. Add celery root and potato slices. Sauté gently for 10 minutes. Season with herbs, salt and pepper. Spread on a cookie sheet. Bake in 350° oven until potato and celery root are tender. Remove from oven; cool.

In a mixing bowl stir together grated cheese and egg yolks, then fold in celery root and potato mixture. Adjust seasoning.

On a clean surface place 3 phyllo sheets on top of each other, brushing each with butter except the top one. Spread evenly with half of celery root mixture then roll into cylindrical shape. Brush with butter and place on cookie sheet. Repeat with remaining phyllo and remaining celery root mixture. Rest 1 hour.

Bake in 400° oven until golden brown on all sides. Cool slightly and slice. Serve with arugula and burnet leaves tossed in vinaigrette.

SPICY PORK POCKETS

Makes 24 pockets; serves 12

For dough, combine flour with salt. Make a well in center; add water and oil. Combine thoroughly for 10 minutes or till dough is smooth and elastic. Place in a bowl and wrap in plastic wrap. Let rest for 1 hour.

For filling, heat oil in sauté pan; add garlic and ginger. Cook over low heat for 1 minute. Add curry powder, vinegar, and salt. Stir gently; add pork. Stir gently, but continuously, over low heat for 15 minutes. Add chicken stock and simmer for 10 minutes. Add cilantro and cumin. Stir and remove from heat; cool.

Divide dough into 24 pieces. Roll out each piece of dough into a 5-inch circle. Cut circles in half. Place 1½ teaspoons of filling in middle of dough. Brush edges of dough with a little water and fold dough around the filling. Fold the edges tightly. Cover with plastic wrap and place in refrigerator for 20 minutes. Fry the pork pockets in hot oil until crispy brown. Remove from oil; drain on paper towels. Serve at once with Papaya, Corn, and Red Pepper Relish.

Dough:

3½ cups	All-purpose flour, sifted
½ teaspoon	Salt
3 tablespoons	Water
1 tablespoon	Olive oil

Filling:

1 tablespoon	Olive oil
2 cloves	Garlic, minced
1 tablespoon	Grated gingerroot
2 tablespoons	Madras curry powder
1 tablespoon	Rice wine vinegar
½ teaspoon	Salt
10 ounces	Pork tenderloin, finely diced
2 tablespoons	Chopped cilantro
⅓ cup	Chicken stock
½ teaspoon	Ground cumin
	Oil for deep-fat frying
	Papaya, Corn, and Red Pepper Relish (*page 66*)

PAN-SEARED LAMB CARPACCIO WITH TUSCAN BEAN SALAD

Serves 6

2	Lamb loins (about 14 ounces), trimmed, no skin or sinew
2 tablespoons	Canola oil
1 teaspoon	Lemon thyme
1 teaspoon	Basil
1 teaspoon	Finely minced garlic
1 teaspoon	Finely minced shallot
1 teaspoon	Mustard seed
½ teaspoon	Dried red pepper flakes
½ teaspoon	Freshly cracked pepper

In a shallow dish, combine lamb with all other ingredients. Marinate for 2 hours. Pan-sear lamb loins on each side until golden brown. Place in 375° oven for 6 minutes. Remove to platter and chill. To serve, slice lamb loin into thin slices and serve over bean salad.

TUSCAN BEAN SALAD

Place cooked beans in a medium mixing bowl. Add diced carrot, celery, red onion, and bell peppers, and combine with oil, vinegar, chives, parsley, salt, and pepper. Marinate for 2 hours prior to serving.

1 cup	Small dried white beans, hulled, soaked, and cooked until tender. Drain, rinse, chill.
1	Large carrot, finely diced
1 stalk	Celery, finely diced
1	Medium red onion, finely diced
1 tablespoon	Finely diced green bell pepper
1 tablespoon	Finely diced red bell pepper
1 tablespoon	Finely diced yellow bell pepper
⅓ cup	Vegetable oil
⅔ cup	Rice wine vinegar
2 tablespoons	Chives
2 tablespoons	Chopped parsley
	Cracked pepper
	Salt

CONFIT OF DUCK

Serves 4

4 tablespoons	Salt
2 tablespoons	Chopped shallots
2 tablespoons	Snipped lemon thyme
2 tablespoons	Cracked white peppercorns
1	Bay leaf, crumbled
2 teaspoons	Minced garlic
1 teaspoon	Mustard seeds
4 tablespoons	Pepper vodka
8 to 10	Duck legs, with thigh meat
4½ cups	Rendered duck fat

In a bowl combine salt, shallots, thyme, peppercorns, bay leaf, garlic, mustard seeds, and vodka. Add duck and rub mixture well into flesh. Cover bowl with plastic wrap and refrigerate for 24 hours. Place duck into clean bowl. Rewrap and refrigerate for 6 more hours.

Heat the rendered fat to 200°. Remove duck from bowl; dry with paper towel. Add duck to hot fat. Cover and cook in a 200° oven about 2½ hours or until tender. Test with wooden pick—it should go into meat with ease. Remove from oven and cool.

Serve with fresh haricots verts tossed with walnut vinaigrette.

RIGATONI IN WILD MUSHROOM BROTH
WITH PARMA HAM AND PORCINI

Serves 6

In a large saucepan, add canola oil and Parma ham and cook over low heat for 1 minute. Add red onion, shallots, and garlic and sauté for 1 minute. Add porcini, morels, shiitakes, and tomato. Deglaze with sherry and add chicken stock. Bring to a boil slowly and reduce to a simmer. Add basil and a little salt and pepper. Add cooked pasta and heat thoroughly. Season to taste. Serve in soup plates. Garnish with Parmesan and basil tips.

3 tablespoons	Canola oil
3 tablespoons	Finely diced Parma ham
1	Medium red onion, finely sliced
1 tablespoon	Minced shallots
1 teaspoon	Minced garlic
3 tablespoons	Finely diced porcini
3 tablespoons	Finely diced morels
3 tablespoons	Finely diced shiitakes
1	Medium tomato, finely diced
⅓ cup	Sherry
1 quart	Chicken stock
3 tablespoons	Snipped basil
	Salt
1 tablespoon	Freshly cracked pepper
1 pound	Rigatoni, cooked in lightly salted water
3 tablespoons	Parmesan

SOUPS

STOCKS

S tocks are probably among the more basic of all culinary techniques and by far they are one of the most crucial elements in many major cooking applications, forming the basis for all soups and sauces and having countless other applications. In fact, a good stock enriches flavor, while adding few calories and very little fat.

Insure its quality by simmering and skimming the stock to maintain clarity. Do not boil the stocks vigorously as this will create an "off" flavor and mostly a cloudy product.

I have included three stock recipes for fish, chicken, and veal. These are by far the most widely used. I encourage you to prepare your own stock from scratch, although there are many commercial products available as substitutes.

FISH STOCK

Makes 2 quarts

Rinse fish bones thoroughly; remove any impurities (blood, etc.) and place in stockpot. Add water, wine, onions, leek, celery, peppercorns, bay leaves, and mustard seed. Bring to a boil; reduce heat and simmer. Skim surface of stock as needed to remove impurities. Simmer for 45 minutes.

Strain stock through fine sieve or cheesecloth; discard bones. Cool stock over ice bath and refrigerate. Stock can be stored in air-tight containers and frozen in small amounts.

5 pounds	Fish bones (preferably flounder, sole, grouper, snapper)
3 quarts	Water
2 cups	White wine
2 large	Onions, cleaned and diced
1 medium	Leek, cleaned and diced
1 medium	Celery stalk, cleaned and diced
1 tablespoon	White peppercorns
4	Bay leaves
1 tablespoon	Mustard seed

CHICKEN STOCK

Makes 2 quarts

Rinse chicken bones thoroughly and add water to bones in a large stockpot. Bring to a boil; reduce heat. Simmer mixture, skimming the surface frequently. Add onion, leeks, celery, cilantro, parsley, and bay leaves, and peppercorns. Simmer stock slowly for 2 hours.

Strain stock through fine sieve or cheesecloth; discard bones. Cool stock over ice bath until cold. Store in refrigerator. Stock can be stored in air-tight containers and frozen in small amounts.

5 pounds	Chicken bones (wings, backs, necks)
3 quarts	Water
3 medium	Onions, diced
2 medium	Leeks, washed and diced
2 medium	Celery stalks, washed and diced
½ bunch	Cilantro
½ bunch	Parsley
3	Bay leaves
1 tablespoon	White peppercorns

BROWN VEAL STOCK

Makes 2 quarts

5 pounds	Veal shank bones, cut into 4-inch pieces
½ cup	Olive oil
4 quarts	Water
3	Carrots, diced
2 stalks	Leeks, diced
3 large	Onions, diced
2 stalks	Celery, diced
10 cloves	Garlic
½ bunch	Cilantro
½ bunch	Parsley
4	Bay leaves
1 tablespoon	Peppercorns
1 tablespoon	Mustard seed
5 ounces	Tomato paste
½ quart	Red wine

Rinse the bones thoroughly and dry with paper towels. Oven roast the bones in roasting pan at 400° until browned. Place bones in stockpot; add water and bring to boiling. Reduce heat to simmer. Meanwhile, in a large skillet heat olive oil and add carrots, leeks, onions, celery, and garlic. Sauté until golden brown. Deglaze pan with red wine. Add tomato paste and stir thoroughly; add to bones in stockpot. Add cilantro, parsley, bay leaves, peppercorns, and mustard seed. Simmer gently for 2½ hours. Strain through fine sieve or cheesecloth; save bones and vegetables. Cool stock over ice bath and refrigerate. Stock can be stored in air-tight containers and frozen in small amounts.

To use the first veal stock, always roast some vegetables, deglaze with red wine and stock, and reduce. This will give the jus more intensity and flavor.

Remouillage
Place reserved bones and vegetables in clean pot; add enough water to just cover and prepare second stock or *remouillage.* Simmer for 2 hours. This stock, although it does not have the same intensity of body and flavor as the first stock, will make a great base stock to start a new stock or as a braising liquid for meats, game, and poultry.

Note: For a variety of stocks use the same preparation but replace veal bone with:

Lamb bones (for lamb stock),
pork bones (for pork stock),
venison bones (for game stock), and
duck bones (for duck stock).

Also, consider using a variety of herbs and spices such as juniper berries for game stock, caraway seed for pork stock, rosemary sprigs for lamb stock, and tarragon for duck stock.

CORN CHOWDER WITH LEEKS
AND BELL PEPPERS

Serves 8

In medium stockpot add oil and sweat (cooking over low heat until translucent and glossy) onion, celery, and leeks for 5 minutes. Add fresh corn, stock, peppercorns, and bay leaf. Simmer over low heat for 35 minutes. Remove from heat and purée mixture in blender. Return to heat and adjust seasoning with herbs, salt, and pepper. Adjust with extra stock if mixture is too thick. Add peppers and cream. Bring to a boil and serve.

5 tablespoons	Olive oil
1 medium	Onion, cleaned and diced
1 stalk	Celery, cleaned and diced
1 stalk	Leek, cleaned and diced
1 pound	Fresh yellow corn kernels
1 quart	Chicken stock
8	Cracked peppercorns
1	Bay leaf
2 tablespoons	Snipped basil
1 tablespoon	Snipped cilantro
1 teaspoon	Snipped thyme leaves
	Salt and pepper
1	Red bell pepper, cleaned, seeded, and finely diced
1	Green bell pepper, cleaned, seeded, and finely diced
½ cup	Heavy cream

SMOKED CHICKEN AND THREE PEPPER SOUP WITH BABY CORN

Serves 8

1 pound	Ground chicken meat
5 large	Egg Whites
2 medium	Carrots, chopped
2 stalks	Celery, chopped
½ cup	Tomatoes, chopped
20	White peppercorns
5	Bay leaves
3 sprigs	Fresh thyme leaves
2 stalks	Leeks, yellow part, chopped
1 tablespoon	Basil
1 tablespoon	Chopped cilantro
6 quarts	Chicken stock, chilled
1 bunch	Cilantro, chopped
1	Smoked chicken carcass, chopped
	Cornbread muffins

Place first eleven ingredients in a heavy stockpot. Add cold stock. Mix thoroughly and bring to a boil slowly. Stir occasionally so that nothing sticks. When mixture reaches boiling point, reduce heat and do not stir. Simmer over very low heat for 1 hour or until consommé is totally clear. Pass consommé through a chinois lined with fine cheesecloth. Keep hot.

Prepare two sachets:
1 with one bunch of washed and chopped cilantro
1 with the chopped carcass of a smoked chicken
Place sachets in consommé and simmer for 45 minutes.
Remove sachets and pass consommé through chinois. Keep hot. Serve with cornbread muffins.
For each serving, place in every soup bowl 1 teaspoon of the following:
Juliennes of:
Smoked chicken, grilled baby corn, red bell pepper, green bell pepper and yellow bell pepper.
Pinch of finely diced serrano pepper
Pinch of pickled ginger and chopped cilantro
Chiffonade of flour tortilla
5 leaves of fresh cilantro

SHRIMP SOUP WITH ROOT VEGETABLES

Serves 6

Melt butter and sauté shallots, garlic, onion, celery, and carrots. Add shrimp and cook for 5 minutes. Add 2 cups wine, bay leaves, and thyme. Simmer for 8 minutes; pour into container and refrigerate overnight.

Remove shrimp from wine mixture, and set aside. Place wine mixture in pot with fish stock and 1 cup wine. Cook on medium-high heat for 15 minutes or until reduced by one third. Add cream and simmer for 10 minutes, stirring frequently. Season with salt and pepper. Add cilantro and shrimp. Heat thoroughly.

In soup bowls place equal amounts of blanched, diced vegetables. Add soup and serve with crusty bread.

4 tablespoons	Butter
2	Shallots, minced
3 cloves	Garlic, minced
1 medium	Onion, sliced
½ cup	Finely diced celery
½ cup	Finely diced carrots
36	Jumbo Gulf shrimp, peeled, deveined, and halved lengthwise
3 cups	Dry white wine
2	Bay leaves
2 sprigs	Fresh Thyme
4 cups	Fish stock
2 cups	Heavy cream
	Salt and pepper
2 tablespoons	Chopped cilantro

One of each, turnip, carrot, celery root, and jicama, finely diced and blanched.

MINTED FISH AND SHELLFISH SOUP WITH CELERIAC

Serves 4

3 tablespoons	Butter
2	Shallots, sliced
¾ cup	Celeriac, julienne
4 ounces	Catfish, cut in strips
4 ounces	Red snapper, cut in strips
	Salt and freshly cracked pepper
4 ounces	Shrimp, peeled and deveined
3 ounces	Mussels, cleaned
4 ounces	Scallops, muscle removed
¾ cup	Dry white wine
2 tablespoons	Pernod
2 tablespoons	Brandy
1¼ cups	Fish stock
4 tablespoons (2 ounces)	Shiitake and hedgehog mushrooms
1	Large tomato, peeled, seeded, and diced
1 tablespoon	Chopped fresh mint

Place butter in saucepan and cook shallots and celeriac until translucent. Season catfish and snapper with salt and pepper and place in saucepan. Add shrimp, mussels, and scallops. Deglaze with white wine, Pernod, and brandy, and simmer for 3 minutes. Remove fish and shellfish and keep warm. Add fish stock and mushrooms and cook for three minutes. Add fish back to stock and simmer over very low heat for five minutes. Add tomato and chopped mint; season with salt and pepper. Serve immediately.

"OH BABY!" SEAFOOD GUMBO

Serves 12

Depending on crawfish season, you might want to substitute pasteurized blue crabmeat. I prefer "Uncle Jerry" Owen's brand spicy sausage.

I n a sauce pot heat oil and sauté sausage about 8 minutes or until brown. Add shallots and garlic. Add onions, celery, and peppers and cook over low heat for 10 minutes. Deglaze with white wine. Add chili sauce, tomato paste, and sassafras and cook for 5 minutes, stirring gently but continuously. Add stock, bring to a boil, and reduce heat to a simmer. Add bay leaf and peppercorns. Add shrimp pieces, catfish strips, and crawfish. Simmer gently for 20 minutes, stirring occasionally to prevent sticking. Season with cilantro, basil, freshly cracked pepper, and a little salt. Add diced tomato and okra until tender. Adjust with additional stock for desired consistency.

5 tablespoons	Safflower oil
½ pound	Ground spicy sausage
6 cloves	Shallots, finely chopped
5 cloves	Garlic, minced
1 cup	Diced onion
1 cup	Diced celery
1 cup	Diced green pepper
½ cup	Diced red pepper
⅓ cup	Dry white wine
⅓ cup	Chili sauce
4 tablespoons	Tomato paste
2½ tablespoons	Ground Sassafras leaves
4 quarts	Fish stock
	Bay leaf and peppercorns
2 pounds	Gulf Shrimp, peeled, deveined, and halved (16 to 20 per pound)
1 pound	Farm-raised catfish fillets, cut into strips
1 cup	Crawfish tails, peeled, deveined, and cooked
4 tablespoons	Chopped cilantro
2 tablespoons	Fresh snipped basil
	Salt and pepper
1 cup	Diced tomato
1 cup	Diced fresh okra

DUCK CONSOMMÉ WITH PORT WINE AND GOLD LEAF

Serves 8 to 12

1 pound	Lean duck meat, ground
12	Egg whites
1 tablespoon	Tomato paste
2	Carrots, minced or finely diced
2 stalks	Celery, minced or finely diced
1	Leek, minced or finely diced
1	Onion, minced or finely diced
8	White peppercorns
8	Mustard seeds
3 sprigs	Fresh thyme
2	Bay leaves
1 sprig	Fresh marjoram
1 sprig	Fresh tarragon
8 cups	Chicken stock, chilled
1 tablespoon	Brandy
6 tablespoons	Port
	Freshly cracked pepper
	Fresh oyster mushrooms, cut into julienne strips
10	Turned and blanched root vegetables (turnip, celeriac, carrot, parsnip, celery, or yam)
10 sheets	Gold Leaf
	Chopped cilantro

In a bowl combine duck meat, egg whites and tomato paste. Add minced vegetables and combine thoroughly. Make sure mixture remains cool, preferably keeping it over ice. Stir in peppercorns, mustard seeds, thyme, bay leaves, marjoram, and tarragon. Fold in the cold stock. Place the mixture in a stock pot and bring to a boil, stirring often. When egg white starts to congeal, reduce heat and simmer slowly for 1½ hours.

Carefully pass consommé through a fine chinois and cheesecloth. Bring soup to a boil slowly, add brandy and port to taste and adjust seasoning. Serve in individual bowls, garnish with mushrooms and root vegetables. Float a sheet of gold leaf on top and sprinkle with chopped cilantro.

PARSNIP AND CARROT SOUP WITH TARRAGON

Serves 6

Heat olive oil in medium stock pot. Add parsnips, carrots, onion, and garlic. Sweat for 2 minutes over low heat, add stock and simmer for 30 minutes.

Blend soup in blender and purée. Return to heat and add cream. Season with salt and pepper and finish with tarragon and a little soft butter. Serve in bowls with garnish of crème fraîche.

3 tablespoons	Olive oil
6	Parsnips, peeled, cleaned, and diced
6	Carrots, peeled, cleaned, and diced
2 small	Red onions, minced
2 cloves	Garlic, minced
4 cups	Chicken stock
½ cup	Heavy cream
	Salt and pepper
1 tablespoon	Chopped tarragon
	Soft butter
	Crème Fraîche

DUTCH SPLIT PEA SOUP

Makes 2 quarts

1 tablespoon	Clarified butter
2	Slices bacon, medium dice
2 tablespoons	Ham, medium dice
1 medium	Onion, medium dice
1	Leek, medium dice
2	Celery stalks, medium dice
1 tablespoon	Minced garlic
8 ounces	Green split peas dried, sorted, and soaked for 24 hours
2 quarts	Chicken stock
1 teaspoon	White pepper
¼ teaspoon	Salt
1	Bay leaf
1 tablespoon	Brandy

In medium sauce pot heat clarified butter over medium heat. Add ham and bacon. Sauté about 2 minutes or until bacon is brown. Add onion, leek, and celery and sweat over low heat for 2 minutes. Add garlic and sweat for 2 more minutes. Add peas and mix well. Add chicken stock, white pepper, salt, and bay leaf. Bring to a boil. Reduce to simmer. Cook for 45 minutes or until peas are soft. Add brandy. Remove from heat and let sit for 10 minutes. Remove bay leaf and blend till smooth. Adjust thickness with additional stock. Season with salt and white pepper, if needed. Serve with crispy bacon and rye bread on the side.

ROMA TOMATO BASIL SOUP

Serves 4

In heavy sauce pot heat olive oil. Add ham and sauté until glossy (1 minute). Add onion and leek and mix well. Sweat for 2 minutes. Add garlic and sweat for 2 minutes. Add tomatoes; mix well. Add chicken stock, salt, and pepper. Bring to a boil. Reduce to simmer. Cook for 30 minutes.

Remove from heat and add basil. Mix well. Let sit for 10 minutes. Blend mixture until smooth. Adjust thickness with additional chicken stock, if needed.

¼ cup	Olive oil
2 ounces	Parma ham, diced
1½ medium	Onions, chopped
1 large	Leek, sliced
1 tablespoon	Minced garlic
10	Roma tomatoes, peeled, seeded, and diced
1½ cups	Chicken stock
½ teaspoon	White pepper
¼ teaspoon	Salt
2 tablespoons	Finely snipped fresh basil

OVEN-ROASTED PLUM TOMATO SOUP WITH CUMINO, CORIANDER, AND AVOCADO PURÉE

Serves 6

20	Plum tomatoes, halved and scored
4 tablespoons	Canola oil
1 tablespoon	Chopped basil leaves
1 tablespoon	Chopped tarragon leaves
1 tablespoon	Chopped parsley
1 quart	Chicken stock
	Freshly cracked pepper
	Salt
1 teaspoon	Coriander powder
1 teaspoon	Cumino powder, or ground cumin
1	Avocado, puréed
1 teaspoon	Chopped cilantro

Place halved tomatoes on baking sheet. Rub tomatoes with oil and sprinkle with basil, tarragon, and parsley. Place tomatoes in 250° oven for 1½ to 2 hours, roasting slowly. Remove tomatoes from oven and purée in vegetable mill. Use all the pulp and skins. Place tomato purée in a stockpot, add chicken stock, and bring to a boil. Season with cracked pepper, coriander, and cumino powder. Combine puréed avocado and chopped cilantro and use to garnish soup.

BLACK BEAN SOUP

Serves 8

Heat oil in large stockpot and add tasso ham. Cook 3 minutes to render ham. Add onions, leeks, celery, and carrots. Cook until tender, about 10 minutes. Add garlic and serrano pepper. Add drained and rinsed beans and stock and bring to a boil. Simmer until beans are tender. Blend mixture and season with cilantro, salt, and pepper. Add a little stock if the consistency is too thick. Serve with Andouille sausage or smoked sausage.

1 tablespoon	Olive oil
4 ounces	Tasso ham, diced
1	Onion, diced
1	Leek, diced
1 stalk	Celery, diced
1	Carrot, diced
2 cloves	Garlic, minced
1	Serrano pepper, seeds removed and chopped
8 ounces	Black beans, sorted and soak overnight
4 quarts	Chicken stock
	Salt and pepper
½ bunch	Cilantro, chopped
	Andouille or smoked sausage

THREE PEPPER GAZPACHO SOUP

Serves 6 to 8

1 medium	Onion
1	Green pepper, seeded
2	Red peppers, seeded
1	Yellow pepper, seeded
2	Cucumbers, seeded
5	Tomatoes, seeded
1 cup	V-8 juice
⅓ cup	Virgin olive oil
⅓ cup	Rice wine vinegar
½ teaspoon	Black pepper
⅛ teaspoon	Salt
½ bunch	Cilantro, chopped
2 tablespoons	Chopped parsley

Grind all vegetables or use food processor and purée coarsely by pulse motion. Remove from bowl and place in mixing bowl. Fold in V-8, oil, and vinegar. Season with cilantro, parsley, pepper, and salt. Serve well chilled.

CHILLED PUMPKIN AND APPLE SOUP

Serves 8

In heavy bottom stockpot heat olive oil. Add onions and leek and cook over low heat for 1 minute. Add pumpkin and apple and cook over low heat for 2 minutes more. Add chicken stock and thyme. Bring mixture to a boil and simmer for 30 minutes. Blend mixture and place into clean pot, bring to a boil and season with sherry, Madeira, salt, pepper, and a little Tabasco. Cool soup base in ice water bath. When cold, add cream. Serve chilled with garnish of chervil leaves and crispy tortilla chips.

⅓ cup	Olive oil
2 medium	Onions, diced
1	Leek, diced
2 cups	Diced pumpkin
2 cups	Diced apples
4 cups	Chicken stock
1 teaspoon	Chopped fresh lemon thyme
2 tablespoons	Madeira
2 tablespoons	Dry sherry
	Salt and Pepper
	Tabasco sauce
1 cup	Light cream
	Chervil leaves
	Tortilla chips

VICTOR'S BEST "RED"

Serves 8 to 12

3 pounds	Red tail venison, coarsely ground
1 pound	Pork butt, coarsely ground
4	Onions, coarsely chopped
16 ounces	Tomato sauce
1 cup	Ginger sherry
4 cloves	Garlic, minced
2 squares	Bitter chocolate
4 tablespoons	Chili powder
4	Jalapeño peppers, diced
4 teaspoons	Cumin seeds
3 teaspoons	Salt
1 teaspoon	Paprika
1 teaspoon	Black pepper
½ teaspoon	Oregano
½ teaspoon	Cayenne pepper
¼ teaspoon	Ground cloves
4 tablespoons	Masa harina (finely ground corn meal)
5	Tomatillos, seeded and diced

If venison is not available, boneless ground chuck or top round will do just fine. The chocolate deepens the color and rounds out the flavor.

Brown meats and onions separately, mix well, and add all other ingredients except masa harina, and tomatillos. Simmer over low heat for one hour stirring occasionally. Just before serving, add tomatillos. Return to heat and stir in masa harina. Combine thoroughly. Serve with cornbread. If too thick, adjust with chicken stock.

SAUCES, RELISHES, AND DRESSINGS

TOMATO MAYONNAISE

Makes 2 cups

Serve with Tartare of Salmon.

8 ounces	Diced tomato
¾ cup	Mayonnaise
4 tablespoons	Tomato paste
1 cup	Chicken stock
	Fresh pepper
	Salt

Combine diced tomato with mayonnaise and tomato paste. Add chicken stock and season with fresh pepper and salt to taste.

CILANTRO DRESSING

Makes 2¼ cups

Serve with Tartare of Salmon.

1 bunch	Cilantro (leaves only)
½ cup	Cold chicken stock
1 cup	Mayonnaise
½ bunch	Cilantro (leaves only), chopped
	Fresh pepper
	Salt

Place 1 bunch cilantro leaves and chicken stock in a blender. Cover and blend till well combined. Place in bowl and stir in mayonnaise and ½ bunch cilantro leaves. Season with fresh pepper and salt.

GREEN APPLE-TOMATILLO SAUCE

Makes about 1 quart

This sauce can be stored for up to 2 days. Before adding the cream, you can freeze the base.

Heat butter in saucepan. Add onion and cook until translucent. Add garlic and jalapeño pepper. Sauté until onion starts to brown; add tomatillos and apples. Add stock and simmer for 30 minutes. Add cilantro and bring to a boil. Blend in a blender. Add heavy cream. Season with salt and pepper. Stir in apple jack and simmer for 10 minutes. Add a little soft butter and blend, then pass through a fine sieve.

4 tablespoons	Clarified butter
1	Medium onion, diced
2 cloves	Garlic, minced
½	Jalapeño pepper, cleaned and chopped
1 pound	Tomatillos, cleaned, washed, and diced
3	Granny Smith apples, cleaned, cored, and diced
1 quart	Chicken stock
1 bunch	Cilantro, coarsely chopped
½ cup	Heavy cream, scalded
	Salt and pepper
¼ cup	Apple jack
	Soft butter

WHITE BEAN MUSTARD SAUCE

Makes 1½ quarts

Great with grilled meats or pan-seared fish. Can also be served as a soup by adjusting the consistency.

½ cup	White beans, picked through, rinsed, and soaked overnight
2	Slices bacon
1 tablespoon	Diced ham
¼ cup	Diced carrots
¼ cup	Diced onions
2 tablespoons	Diced leeks
2 teaspoons	Minced garlic
2	Serrano peppers, minced
¼ cup	Clarified butter
2 quarts	Chicken stock
1 teaspoon	Salt
1 teaspoon	White pepper
1	Bay leaf
2 tablespoons	Brandy
2 tablespoons	Dijon mustard
1 tablespoon	Fresh chopped lemon thyme

In stock pot heat butter. Add bacon and ham and cook over low heat for 1 minute. Add carrots, onions, and leeks. Mix well and cook over low heat for 10 minutes. Add garlic and serrano peppers. Mix well. Cook over low heat for 3 more minutes. Add beans and stock. Mix well. Stir in salt, white pepper, and bay leaf. Bring to a boil. Reduce heat and cook for 45 minutes or until beans are soft. Add brandy, mustard, and thyme. Mix well. Turn off heat and let sit for 10 minutes. Remove bay leaf. Place mixture in a blender. Cover and blend till smooth. Return to a clean pot. Bring to a boil. Reduce heat and simmer. Adjust thickness and seasoning, if needed. Cook for 5 minutes and serve with grilled meats or fish.

PEANUT SAUCE

Makes about 2 cups (makes 1 pound of base)

Delicious with roast pork or steak.

In large skillet or wok heat oil. Cook shallots and garlic in hot oil. Add serrano chilies, teriyaki sauce, red pepper flakes, shrimp paste, and lemon juice. Remove from heat and place in mixing bowl; cool mixture. When cool, stir in peanut butter. Stir in sugar.

Store in container in refrigerator. Can be kept for 2 to 3 weeks. To use the sauce, combine 1 part peanut sauce with 3 parts chicken stock. Heat thoroughly and serve. Adjust seasoning with salt or pepper.

6 tablespoons	Peanut oil
3 tablespoons	Minced shallots
½ tablespoon	Minced garlic
3	Serrano chilies
2 tablespoons	Teriyaki sauce
1 tablespoon	Red pepper flakes
1 tablespoon	Shrimp paste
1 tablespoon	Lemon juice
1 pound	Crunchy peanut butter
2 tablespoons	Brown sugar
	Chicken stock

DEVILED CORN AND TOMATO SALSA

Makes about 1½ cups

A refreshing salsa for grilled chicken, steak, or fish.

1 cup	Fresh yellow corn kernels, cooked
2	Roma tomatoes, peeled, seeded, and diced
1 small	Jicama, peeled and diced
1 small	Green pepper, diced
1 small	Onion, finely chopped
2 cloves	Garlic, finely minced
1	Jalapeño pepper, seeded and finely chopped
1 teaspoon	Finely grated gingerroot
3 tablespoons	Fresh grapefruit juice
2 tablespoons	Rice wine vinegar
1 tablespoon	Sesame oil
4 tablespoons	Finely chopped cilantro
½ teaspoon	Ground cumin
	Salt and pepper

In a bowl combine corn, diced tomatoes, jicama, pepper, and onion. Add minced garlic, jalapeño pepper, and gingerroot; toss well. Add grapefruit juice, vinegar, oil, cilantro, and cumin. Season with salt and pepper.

GREEN APPLE-TOMATILLO RELISH

Makes about 4 cups

Good with spring or summer salads, serve it also as an accompaniment to grilled fish (especially salmon), pork, and sautéed items. It tastes best after overnight refrigeration.

Combine tomatillos, jicama, apples, and peppers. In a mixing bowl combine vinegar, orange juice, lime juice, and garlic. Slowly mix in olive oil. Toss with tomatillo mixture and season with cilantro, salt, and pepper. Marinate for 1 hour.

1 pound	Tomatillos, diced
2 cups	Diced jicama
1 cup	Diced green apples
5 tablespoons	Diced red bell pepper
5 tablespoons	Diced yellow bell pepper
1	Jalapeño pepper, seeded and finely chopped
½ cup	Rice wine vinegar
1	Orange, juiced
1	Lime, juiced
3 cloves	Garlic, minced
1 cup	Virgin olive oil
½ cup	Chopped cilantro
	Salt and pepper

OLIVE AND TOMATO RELISH

Makes about 1½ cups

Serve with grilled or sautéed fish or meats.

1 tablespoon	Olive oil
1 tablespoon	Minced shallots
3 cloves	Garlic, minced
½ tablespoon	Brown sugar
2 large	Tomatoes, seeded and diced
¼ cup	Sliced black olives
1 tablespoon	Raspberry vinegar
½ teaspoon	Snipped thyme leaves
½ teaspoon	Snipped marjoram leaves
	Salt and pepper

In saucepan heat olive oil; add shallots, garlic, and sugar. Cook gently for 1 minute. Add tomatoes and olives; simmer over low heat for 20 minutes. Add vinegar, thyme, and marjoram. Adjust seasoning with salt and pepper.

RED ONION AND APPLE RELISH

Makes about 2 cups

This is my adaptation of a classical onion brûlee. Serve with steamed or braised fish or roast pork.

In saucepan stir together port, red wine, and sugar. Add onions and apples and bring to a rapid boil. Reduce heat and simmer until liquid is almost evaporated. Season with salt and pepper.

½ cup	Port wine
⅓ cup	Red wine
½ tablespoon	Sugar
3	Red onions, thinly sliced
2	Green apples, cleaned, cored, and sliced in strips
	Salt and pepper

PAPAYA-TOMATO RELISH

Makes 2 cups

In medium bowl combine papaya, tomato, parsley, chives, gherkins, red pepper, and capers. In small bowl combine vinegar and garlic. Whisk in olive oil and blend well. Pour over papaya mixture; toss to coat. Add salt and pepper to taste.

1 medium	Papaya, diced
⅓ cup	Diced tomato (1 medium)
¼ cup	Chopped parsley
¼ cup	Chopped chives
¼ cup	Chopped sweet gherkins
¼ cup	Diced red pepper
3 tablespoons	Small capers
¼ cup	Rice wine vinegar
1 large clove	Garlic, minced
⅓ cup	Virgin olive oil
	Salt and pepper

PAPAYA, CORN, AND RED PEPPER RELISH

Makes about 2 cups

A mouthwatering relish that's superb with grilled swordfish or pan-seared steak or chicken.

1 cup	**Diced papaya**
⅓ cup	**Diced fresh pineapple**
⅓ cup	**Diced red bell pepper**
⅓ cup	**Roasted corn kernels**
⅓ cup	**Olive oil**
⅓ cup	**Rice wine vinegar**
2 tablespoons	**Chopped cilantro**
1	**Serrano pepper, seeded and finely chopped**
1 tablespoon	**Lemon juice**
	Fresh cracked pepper
	Salt

Stir together papaya, pineapple, red bell pepper, corn, olive oil, vinegar, cilantro, serrano pepper, and lemon juice. Season with pepper and a little salt. Let stand for 1 hour before serving.

CRANBERRY AND BLUEBERRY RELISH

Makes about 1½ cups

This sweet and zesty relish stores well in the refrigerator. Serve chilled with spicy sausage or pâtés.

Combine cranberries, blueberry preserves, blueberries, orange peel, orange juice, lime peel, lime juice, basil, brandy, and vinegar. Season with salt and pepper.

½ pound	Cranberries, finely chopped
½ cup	Blueberry preserves
½ cup	Blueberries
2	Oranges, fine zest and juice
1	Lime, fine zest and juice
3 tablespoons	Chopped basil
3 tablespoons	Brandy
2 tablespoons	Balsamic vinegar
	Salt and pepper

CREAMY VINAIGRETTE

Makes about 2½ cups

You can use a little stock or boullion to thin out the vinaigrette if desired. Store in glass bottles and keep refrigerated.

In mixing bowl whisk egg yolks. Add mustard and whisk until frothy. Slowly add olive oil while continuing to whisk. Add shallots; whisk in vinegar. Adjust seasoning with salt and pepper.

4	Egg yolks
½ cup	Dijon mustard
1½ cups	Virgin olive oil
1 tablespoon	Minced shallots
½ cup	Rice wine vinegar
	Salt and pepper

BASIL AND CHIVE VINAIGRETTE

Makes about 4 cups

This vinaigrette will store for up to a week in the refrigerator. Keep in a tightly closed container. Serve with arugula salads, asparagus, braised and chilled celery, or Belgium endive.

1½ cups	Virgin olive oil
2 cups	Rice wine vinegar
1 medium	Red onion, diced
1	Yellow pepper, finely diced
2	Hard-boiled eggs, chopped
2 tablespoons	Chopped parsley
2 tablespoons	Snipped basil
2 tablespoons	Snipped chives
1 tablespoon	Dijon mustard
1 teaspoon	Worcestershire sauce
½ teaspoon	Salt
½ teaspoon	Cracked peppercorns

In large mixing bowl combine all ingredients. Mix well.

SMOKEY CITRUS VINAIGRETTE

Makes about 2½ cups

This different and exciting vinaigrette stores well in the refrigerator. Try it with cold roast pork loin and cucumber salad—or with tart greens.

½ cup	Rice wine vinegar
3 tablespoons	Brown sugar
1 tablespoon	Dijon mustard
¼ cup	Barbeque sauce
5 tablespoons	Maple syrup
1½ cups	Olive oil
1	Orange, juiced
1	Lemon, juiced
1 tablespoon	Liquid barbeque smoke
	Freshly cracked pepper

In blender place vinegar, sugar, and mustard, and blend on medium speed for 5 minutes. Add the barbeque sauce and maple syrup. Blend for 3 more minutes. Slowly add olive oil, a little at a time, while blender is running. Add orange juice, lemon juice, and liquid smoke.

Season with freshly cracked pepper.

PARSLEY AND WATERCRESS CREAMY VINAIGRETTE

Makes about 4 cups

Use as dressing for haricot verts or as a sauce for carpaccio.

Combine egg yolks, mustard, garlic, and half of the lemon juice. Blend ingredients thoroughly. Whisk until ribbons form. Slowly incorporate the oil, whisking continuously until all the oil is well combined. Add chicken stock and remaining lemon juice. Stir in cream. Season with peppercorns, cognac, and salt. Fold in the puréed parsley and watercress.

6	Egg yolks
2 tablespoons	Dijon mustard
4 cloves	Garlic, minced
4	Lemons, juiced
1½ cups	Cottonseed oil
1 cup	Chicken stock
½ cup	Heavy cream
4 tablespoons	Cracked peppercorns
4 tablespoons	Cognac
	Salt
2 bunches	Parsley cleaned, stems removed, chopped and puréed
2 bunches	Watercress, cleaned and stems removed

ANCHOVY CAPER DRESSING

Makes about 2 cups

Try with marinated salmon or a classical Niçoise salad.

1 cup	**Virgin olive oil**
¾ cup	**Rice wine vinegar**
8	**Anchovies, minced**
⅓ cup	**Chopped gherkins**
4 tablespoons	**Chopped parsley**
4 tablespoons	**Chopped chives**
3 cloves	**Garlic, minced**
2 tablespoons	**Small capers**
½	**Lemon, juiced**
	Salt and pepper

Stir together oil, vinegar, anchovies, gherkins, parsley, chives, garlic, capers, and lemon juice. Adjust seasoning with salt and pepper. Serve on pasta salad or lettuce.

BASIL PESTO

Makes ½ cup

5 cloves	**Garlic**
½ cup	**Chopped basil**
½ cup	**Parmesan cheese**
1 tablespoon	**Olive oil**

In a blender or food processor combine garlic and basil. Cover and blend till well combined. Add Parmesan cheese and olive oil. Cover and blend till mixture forms a paste. Toss with cooked pasta.

MARMALADE OF ONION WITH GRENADINE

Serves 6 to 8

Serve with grilled meats, fish, or roasts.

Heat olive oil in saucepan; add onions and cook and stir until glossy. Add sugar and caramelize. Deglaze with wine. Add orange juice, orange zest, Grenadine syrup, and vinegar. Cook gently until onions are tender.

3 tablespoons	Olive oil
½ pound	Onions, sliced
4 tablespoons	Brown sugar
⅓ cup	Liberty School Cabernet Sauvignon or dry red wine
1	Orange, peel finely shredded and juiced
2 tablespoons	Grenadine syrup
1 tablespoon	Rice wine vinegar

APRICOT AND PRUNE CHUTNEY

Makes about 3 cups

If using dried apricots and prunes, bloom in ¾ cup chicken stock—to plump. This chutney stores well in the refrigerator.

¾ cup	Chicken stock
½ pound	Apricots, cleaned and quartered
½ pound	Prunes, cleaned and quartered
3 tablespoons	Virgin olive oil
8 cloves	Shallots, minced
8 cloves	Garlic, minced
¼ cup	Freshly grated gingerroot
½ cup	Orange juice
1 teaspoon	Orange zest
⅓ cup	Rice wine vinegar
⅓ cup	Cranberry juice
1 bunch	Cilantro, chopped
1 teaspoon	Ground nutmeg
1 teaspoon	Ground cinnamon
⅓ cup	Maple syrup

Bloom apricots and prunes in chicken stock. In saucepan heat olive oil. Add shallots, garlic, and gingerroot and cook for 1 minute over low heat. Add orange juice, peel, vinegar, and cranberry juice; bring to a boil. Simmer for 15 minutes. Add apricots and prunes. Season with cilantro, nutmeg, and cinnamon. Add syrup. Simmer gently for 15 minutes more. Cool and serve with grilled meats and or fish.

LINGONBERRY AMARETTO SAUCE

Makes about 1½ cups

Serve with duck sausages and creamed orzo and leeks.

In saucepan caramelize sugar with half of the butter. Add red wine, orange juice, and lingonberries and reduce by two-thirds. Add jus and reduce by one-third. Add amaretto and mustard. Season with salt and pepper and finish with remaining butter.

1 tablespoon	Sugar
6 tablespoons	Butter
2 cups	Dry red wine
⅓ cup	Orange juice
2 tablespoons	Lingonberries
2 cups	Brown jus (duck or fowl)
⅓ cup	Amaretto di Saronno
1 tablespoon	Mustard
	Salt and pepper

BLOOD ORANGE-CILANTRO CREAM

Makes about ¾ cup, Serves 6 to 8

Well suited for any grilled, poached, or pan-seared fish.

½ cup	Fish stock
3	Blood oranges, juiced
2 tablespoons	Chopped cilantro
1	Shallot, finely chopped
½ cup	Heavy cream
1	Bay leaf
8	White peppercorns, cracked
2 tablespoons	butter

In saucepan simmer stock, blood orange juice and shallot over low heat until reduced by one-fourth. Add cream, bay leaf, and peppercorns and simmer for 10 minutes. Strain through fine sieve and whisk in butter. Blend in blender for 10 seconds and keep warm until needed.

ENTREES

THREE-NUT-CRUSTED PORK TENDERLOIN

Serves 6

This, accompanied by Green Apple-Tomatillo Relish, won the National Pork Producer's Council Award in 1988. With these savory pork mignons I like to serve Caymus Conundrum 1989, a wonderful blend of Chardonnay and Semillion blanc.

12 3-ounce	**Mignons fresh pork tenderloin**
	Salt
	Freshly cracked pepper
½ cup	**Flour**
3	**Eggs, lightly beaten**
½ cup	**Finely chopped hazelnuts**
½ cup	**Finely chopped pecans**
1 cup	**Bread crumbs, toasted**
1 cup	**All Bran flakes**
½ cup	**Finely chopped macadamia nuts, toasted**
⅓ cup	**Olive oil**
⅓ cup	**Clarified butter**

Season pork mignons with salt and freshly cracked pepper. Dust with flour and dip in beaten eggs. Combine bread crumbs, bran, and nuts. Coat pork in nut mixture and set aside. Heat large skillet; add olive oil and butter and sauté pork mignons until golden brown on all sides. Bake in 350° oven for about 5 minutes. Serve at once.

GRILLED PORK SATÉ

Serves 6

Serve with Asahi beer, super dry.

Place all ingredients except pork and Peanut Sauce in blender. Blend thoroughly and set aside.

Remove skewers from packet and soak in water for a little more than 1 hour prior to use (this will prevent the skewers from burning while cooking the pork). Thread pork on skewers. Place in shallow dish and rub marinade over pork. Marinate for 2 hours, turning twice to insure optimum flavor.

Grill the pork on a moderately heated grill for about 15 minutes, turning frequently. Serve at once with Peanut Sauce.

2 pounds	Pork tenderloin, cut into 1-inch cubes
3 large	Shallots, finely diced
3 cloves	Garlic, finely minced
2 teaspoons	Finely grated fresh gingerroot
⅓ cup	Saki wine
2 tablespoons	Dried red pepper flakes
½ teaspoon	Salt
3 tablespoons	Olive oil
1 teaspoon	Brown sugar
1 bag	6-inch Bamboo skewers
	Peanut Sauce *(page 61)*

SAUTÉED PORK TENDERLOIN WITH LIMA BEAN MUSTARD SAUCE

Serves 8

Maple Apples (p. 122) makes a splendid accompanying dish. Try with William Hill Williamette White Riesling 1989.

Sauce Preparation

3 tablespoons	Virgin olive oil
4 ounces	Tasso ham
2 cloves	Garlic, minced
1	Onion, diced
1	Leek, diced
1 stalk	Celery, diced
1	Carrot, diced
1	Red pepper, cleaned, seeded, and diced
1	Green pepper, cleaned, seeded, and diced
½ pound	Lima beans (soaked overnight)
1 tablespoon	Dijon mustard
	Chicken stock
	Salt and pepper
½ tablespoon	Snipped fresh tarragon
	Soft butter
	Clarified butter
8 6-ounce	Pieces pork tenderloin, trimmed, sinew removed

In a saucepan, heat olive oil. Add ham and cook over low heat (sweat) for 5 minutes. Add garlic, onion, leek, celery, carrots, and peppers. Cook over low heat until soft, about 10 minutes. Add beans and cover with chicken stock. Cook about 30 minutes or until beans are tender.

Purée mixture with blender then pass through a sieve. Return sauce to saucepan. Add Dijon mustard and season with a little salt and pepper and adjust consistency with chicken stock. Finish with freshly snipped tarragon and soft butter.

Pork Preparation

In a skillet, heat butter and sauté pork tenderloin until golden brown on all sides. Place in 375° oven and continue cooking for 5 minutes. Allow meat to rest before slicing. Serve with Lima Bean Mustard Sauce and Maple Apples.

LIMA BEAN MUSTARD SAUCE

Makes 1 quart

This sauce is great with any pork dish.

Rinse the soaked beans in a colander and drain well. In a saucepan heat olive oil and cook leeks, onions, and garlic over low heat until translucent. Add beans and chicken stock and bring to a boil. Reduce heat and simmer slowly for 45 minutes. Add bay leaves, peppercorns, and mustard seeds and simmer gently for 30 minutes. Add mustard, sherry, Pernod, basil, and lemon thyme. Remove bay leaves. Blend in a blender and pass through a sieve. Return to a boil and adjust seasoning; keep warm. Adjust with stock to achieve proper consistency.

1 cup	Dried baby lima beans, soaked overnight
1½ tablespoons	Olive oil
⅓ cup	Diced leeks
⅓ cup	Diced onion
2 cloves	Garlic, minced
6 cups	Chicken stock
2	Bay leaves
½ tablespoon	Peppercorns
1 teaspoon	Mustard seed
2 tablespoons	Creole mustard
2 tablespoons	Dry sherry
2 tablespoons	Pernod
1 tablespoon	Snipped Opal basil
½ tablespoon	Snipped lemon thyme

PORK AND TWO BEAN CASSOULET

Serves 8

Serve with Buehler White Zinfandel, Napa 1990; or Bonny Doon Vin Gris de Cigare, Santa Cruz 1990.

4 pounds	Pork butt, cleaned of sinew and excess fat
2	Bay leaves
1 tablespoon	Snipped lemon thyme
6 cloves	Garlic, minced
1 tablespoon	Cracked peppercorns
⅓ cup	Olive oil
½ pound	Parma ham, diced
⅓ pound	Red onions, diced
½ cup	Diced leeks
4 quarts	Chicken stock
1 cup	Red wine
½ cup	Madeira
½ cup	White beans (soaked overnight in water)
½ cup	Black beans (soaked overnight in water)
1 pound	Roma tomatoes, peeled, seeded, and diced
½ bunch	Cilantro, chopped
	Salt and pepper

Cut pork butt into 1-inch cubes and place in large bowl. Add bay leaves, thyme, garlic, and peppercorns; combine thoroughly. Marinate in refrigerator for 2 hours.

In a heavy pot heat half of the olive oil; add Parma ham and cook over low heat for 2 minutes. Add onions and leeks and sauté for 3 minutes, stirring frequently. Add half of the chicken stock. Bring to a boil and reduce to a simmer.

In heavy sauté pan, heat remaining olive oil and quickly sear pork. Add to the Parma ham, leek, and onion mixture and deglaze with red wine and Madeira. Simmer slowly for ½ hour, adding chicken stock if mixture reduces too much.

Add beans and cook slowly for an additional ½ hour, stirring occasionally. Add tomatoes and cilantro. Adjust seasoning with a touch of salt and pepper. Taste beans, they should be tender but still retain their shape.

Serve at once.

GRILLED PORK MEDALLIONS WITH BRAISED FLAGEOLETS, ZUCCHINI, AND SQUASH

Serves 6

I serve this with 1989 Domaine Weinbach, Cuvée Theo.

Heat oil in a medium saucepan. Add diced leeks and cook over low heat for 1 minute. Deglaze pan with Madeira. Add stock, tarragon, and parsley. Add prepared beans and simmer over low heat for 20 minutes, stirring occasionally. Add diced tomatoes, season with salt and pepper and keep warm.

Sauté zucchini and squash briefly in a little stock and season with salt and pepper.

Grill pork medallions on a moderately hot grill until medium and keep hot.

Arrange zucchini and squash in a circle on each plate. Place flageolets in the center of the plate and place the pork medallion on top of the beans.

Serve at once.

2 tablespoons	Canola oil
1 stalk	Leeks, white part diced
⅓ cup	Madeira, or dry red wine
2 cups	Chicken stock
1½ tablespoons	Snipped tarragon
1½ tablespoons	Chopped parsley
1 pound	Flageolet beans, hulled, cleaned, soaked, and cooked in lightly salted water
4	Tomatoes, diced, flesh only
	Salt
	Pepper
2	Zucchinis, julienne
2	Yellow squashes, julienne
6 5-ounce	Center cut pork medallions, trimmed, excess fat removed

GRILLED PORK LOIN IN APRICOT AND CURRY MARINADE

Serves 8

Either Firestone Santa Barbara (1985–89) or Rutherford Hill Gewurtraminers are fine here.

8 7-ounce	Center cuts of fresh, boneless pork loin
2 cups	Finely sliced onions
1 cup	Smooth apricot jam
½ cup	Balsamic vinegar
½ cup	Olive oil
⅓ cup	V-8 juice
⅓ cup	Brandy
4 tablespoons	Worcestershire sauce
2 tablespoons	Chopped lemongrass
1 tablespoon	Brown sugar
15	White peppercorns, cracked
4 cloves	Garlic, minced
4	Bay leaves
1 teaspoon	Grated fresh gingerroot
½ teaspoon	Madras curry powder

Place pork in stainless steel or enamel bowl. Combine remaining ingredients well to make marinade. Pour over pork. Cover and chill in refrigerator for 1 day, turning pork occasionally. (To achieve more intense flavor, marinate 1½ days.)

Remove pork from marinade and grill on both sides until browned. Finish in a 375° oven for 5 minutes. Do not overcook.

RED SNAPPER DUMPLINGS WITH JICAMA AND MUSHROOMS

Serves 4

Try with Preston Cuvee de Fume, Dry Creek Fume Blanc 1989.

Cut red snapper in small cubes and place in bowl over ice. In chilled food processor purée snapper meat till fine and smooth. Add egg whites; place in bowl over ice. Fold in cream, Noilly Pratt, chives, basil, and thyme. Season with salt and pepper.

Test snapper mixture for flavor by poaching in a little fish stock. Adjust seasoning. Shape into dumplings. In well-seasoned fish stock, poach dumplings for 2 to 3 minutes or until firm to the touch.

In saucepan heat olive oil. Add gingerroot, shallots, serrano pepper, and cook over low heat until glossy. Deglaze with brandy. Add mushrooms and jicama. Simmer over low heat. Add fish stock. Cook slowly for 5 minutes; adjust seasoning with salt and pepper. Serve with dumplings.

1 pound	Red snapper (center cut, skin and gristle removed)
2	Egg whites
⅓ cup	Heavy cream
4 tablespoons	Noilly Pratt or any dry vermouth
1 tablespoon	Snipped fresh chives
1 tablespoon	Snipped fresh basil
½ tablespoon	Snipped lemon thyme
	Salt and pepper
⅓ cup	Fish stock
1 tablespoon	Olive oil
1 tablespoon	Minced gingerroot
2	Shallots, chopped
1	Serrano pepper, chopped
⅓ cup	Brandy
½ pound	Mushrooms
⅓ pound	Jicama, diced and blanched

PAN-SEARED SNAPPER ON CURRIED ROASTED VEGETABLES

Serves 6

A suggested wine is William Wheeler 1988 Reserve, red table wine.

6 6-ounce	Red snapper fillets (cleaned, boneless, skinless)
	Salt and pepper
	Flour
6 tablespoons	Olive oil

Lightly season red snapper with salt and pepper. Dust with flour and pan sauté in oil until browned on both sides. Place in oven at 350° for 5 to 7 minutes or until fish just flakes.

CURRIED ROASTED VEGETABLES

½ tablespoon	Olive oil
1	Red onion, minced
3 cloves	Garlic, minced
½ tablespoon	Madras curry powder
½ cup	Julienned jicama
½ cup	Julienned carrots
½ cup	Julienned leeks
½ cup	Julienned celery
2 tablespoons	Teriyaki sauce
2 tablespoons	Chopped cilantro
	Salt

In sauté pan heat olive oil, add onion and garlic, sweat for 1 minute over low heat. Add curry powder and sauté gently until onion is glossy. Add jicama, carrots, leeks, and celery and sauté over high heat for 1 minute. Finish cooking in oven at 350° for 10 to 15 minutes. Remove from oven and add teriyaki sauce, cilantro, and a little salt. Combine and place on serving platter. Arrange snapper fillets on top and serve at once.

RED SNAPPER WITH CRAYFISH IN CORNBREAD CRUST

Serves 6

Try 1989 Talbott Monterey with this delectable snapper.

Place portioned snapper on serving plate. Stir together oil, cilantro, seasoning, serrano pepper, and pepper. Carefully spread over snapper fillets. Cover and marinate snapper for 4 hours in the refrigerator.

Preheat oven to 400°.

For the cornbread crust, in a medium sauté pan heat olive oil. Place crayfish, tomatillos, jicama, and chayote squash on a plate and sprinkle with paprika. Add mixture to hot oil and sauté about 3 minutes. Deglaze with brandy. Remove mixture to bowl and let cool. Once mixture is cool, add grated cornbread. Mix well and set aside.

Remove marinated snapper from marinade. Season with salt and fresh cracked pepper. In large sauté pan heat clarified butter. Once pan is hot, place marinated snapper in pan, flesh side down. Sear for 30 to 60 seconds. Turn over and sear other side for 30 to 60 seconds. Place snapper in preheated 400° oven for 5 to 6 minutes or until snapper just flakes. Remove snapper from oven. Place loose layer of cornbread mixture over snapper. Place under broiler and crisp for 30 seconds. Remove and serve with White Bean Mustard Sauce.

6 5-ounce	Red snapper fillets (cleaned, boneless, skinless)
¼ cup	Extra virgin olive oil
2 tablespoons	Finely chopped cilantro
1 tablespoon	Cajun blackening seasoning
1	Serrano pepper, seeded and minced
½ teaspoon	Black pepper
¼ cup	Olive oil
6 ounces	Crayfish tails, cooked, cleaned, and diced or 6 ounces cooked crabmeat, diced
2	Tomatillos, washed, cleaned, and diced
1 medium	Jicama, peeled, cleaned, and diced
1 medium	Chayote squash, peeled, cleaned, and diced
1 tablespoon	Paprika
2 tablespoons	Brandy
8 ounces	Cornbread, grated
	Salt
	Freshly cracked pepper
¼ cup	Clarified butter
	White Bean Mustard Sauce (page 60)

TURBOT, SCALLOPS AND PRAWNS IN AMARETTO SAFFRON BROTH

Serves 6

Serve with Spottswoode Sauvignon Blanc, Napa 1989–90.

1 quart	Fish stock
3 tablespoons	Finely diced tomato, no pulp, no skin
	Sachet with bay leaf, peppercorn, and mustard seed
⅛ teaspoon	Saffron threads
2 tablespoons	Amaretto
6 3-ounce	Turbot fillets
	Salt and pepper
	Flour
⅓ cup	Virgin olive oil
12	Sea scallops, muscle removed
6	Prawns, peeled and cleaned
	Pre-prepared root vegetables such as turnips, parsnips, carrots, fennel, and celery
2 tablespoons	Chopped parsley
2 tablespoons	Snipped basil

Combine fish stock, tomato concassee and sachet. Simmer over low heat. Keep warm. Meanwhile, steep the saffron with the Amaretto. Set aside. Season turbot with salt and pepper and dust with flour. Lightly sauté in olive oil. Sear both sides. Repeat procedure with sea scallops and prawns; set aside. Divide root vegetables evenly among large soup plates. Add fish, scallops, and prawns to bowls; set bowls in 150° to 200° oven and heat thoroughly. Add steeped saffron to fish stock. Just before serving, top seafood medley with saffron broth. Garnish with parsley and basil. Serve at once.

SHALLOW-BAKED GROUPER WITH BOK CHOY IN MAPLE-SESAME DRESSING

Serves 8

Serve with Ferrari-Carano Alexander Chardonnay 1989.

Cook crawfish in boiling water; keep warm. Brush large, shallow sauté pan with butter; add mushrooms and shallots. Place fish fillets on top and add fish stock, brandy, and wine. Sprinkle with a little salt and freshly ground pepper. Cover with buttered parchment paper and place in 375° oven for 8 minutes or just until fish flakes. Remove fish. Reduce pan drippings, strain over fish fillets and garnish with crawfish tails. Serve with honey-sesame dressed bok choy.

½ cup	Fresh crawfish tails, peeled, deveined
1 tablespoon	Butter
½ cup	Sliced mushrooms
2 tablespoons	Finely chopped shallots
8 6-ounce	Boneless grouper fillets, skinned
¾ cup	Fish stock
4 tablespoons	Brandy
4 tablespoons	Dry white wine
	Salt
1 tablespoon	Freshly cracked pepper

BOK CHOY IN MAPLE-SESAME DRESSING

Makes about ½ cup

Combine all ingredients thoroughly. Drizzle over cooked bok choy and serve.

2 tablespoons	Maple syrup
2 tablespoons	Rice wine vinegar
2 tablespoons	Fish stock
1 tablespoon	Sesame seeds, toasted
1 tablespoon	Olive oil
1 teaspoon	Chopped cilantro
¼ teaspoon	Ground cumin
Pinch	Freshly cracked pepper
8 stalks	Bok choy, cooked

FILLET OF SALMON IN BRIOCHE CRUST AND PORCINI SAUCE

Serves 6

Try Etude Pinot Noir, Napa 1989.

6 7-ounce	Boneless, skinless salmon fillets
4 tablespoons	Okhotnichya vodka
1 tablespoon	Chopped cilantro
1 tablespoon	Chopped basil
1 tablespoon	Ground pepper
¾ cup	Bran flakes cereal, crushed
¾ cup	Brioche bread crumbs
½ cup	Crushed pecans
3 tablespoons	Chopped parsley
4 tablespoons	Clarified butter
3 tablespoons	Virgin olive oil
	Porcini Sauce

Marinate salmon in vodka, cilantro, basil, and pepper. Set in refrigerator for 1 hour. Meanwhile, combine bran flakes, bread crumbs, pecans, parsley, and butter; set aside.

In large saucepan heat olive oil and pan-sear salmon fillets on one side only till browned. Reduce heat and continue cooking for 3 minutes; do not turn salmon. Place salmon on small sheetpan and place in 350° oven for 4 minutes. Remove from oven and coat each steak with pecan-bran mixture. Broil until evenly browned. Serve at once with Porcini Sauce.

PORCINI SAUCE

Makes about 2 cups

A good sauce with salmon or grilled meats. If using a commercial stock, reduce it longer.

I n medium saucepan cook shallots and garlic in butter until glazed. Add diced porcini and deglaze with Merlot. Cook over low heat. Add veal stock and veal jus; simmer over low heat for 15 minutes. Blend mixture in blender, and pass through a fine sieve. Place in small saucepan and finish sauce over low heat with salt and pepper and a little soft butter. Keep warm till needed. Serve with salmon steaks.

2	Shallots, finely diced
2 cloves	Garlic, finely minced
1 tablespoon	Butter
6 ounces	Porcini mushrooms (fresh or frozen), diced
6 tablespoons	Rutherford Hill Merlot or dry red wine
1 cup	Veal stock (*p. 42*)
1 cup	Veal jus
	Salt and pepper
	Soft butter

PAN-SEARED SALMON WITH GREEN LENTIL COMPOTE

Serves 6

The Green Lentil Compote is a versatile accompaniment. Try it also with Pheasant Parcel in Phyllo (p. 101). A suggested wine here is Chateau Montelena Chardonnay 1989.

6 7-ounce	Boneless, skinless salmon fillets
1 tablespoon	Snipped fresh basil
1 tablespoon	Snipped fresh lemon thyme
½ teaspoon	Snipped fresh rosemary
½ teaspoon	Cracked black pepper
½ cup	Clarified butter

Rub salmon with herbs and pepper; marinate for at least 1 hour in the refrigerator.

In a skillet heat clarified butter. Sauté salmon fillets, skin side down, until brown. Do not turn. Remove from heat, pour off some of the butter and bake in 350° oven until the salmon is moist inside and crisp on the bottom.

Serve on Green Lentil Compote.

GREEN LENTIL COMPOTE

Serves 6 to 8

D rain lentils in colander and rinse. Cook lentils in chicken stock about 30 minutes or until tender but still firm; drain. Spread on baking sheet to cool quickly.

Cook shallots, gingerroot, serrano pepper, and garlic in butter over low heat until glazed. Add corn and jicama and cook for 2 minutes. Add lentils and bell pepper and sauté gently over low heat. Season with cilantro, basil, freshly cracked pepper, and a little salt. Keep warm until needed.

1 pound	Green lentils, soaked overnight in cold water to cover
1½ quarts	Chicken stock
1 tablespoon	Minced shallots
1 teaspoon	Minced gingerroot
½	Serrano pepper, chopped
1 teaspoon	Minced garlic
1 tablespoon	Butter
3 tablespoons	Fresh corn
3 tablespoons	Diced jicama
3 tablespoons	Diced red bell pepper
2 tablespoons	Chopped cilantro
1 tablespoon	Chopped fresh basil
	Freshly cracked pepper
	Salt

PECAN- AND BRAN-CRUSTED CATFISH

Serves 6

Try Fall Creek Emerald Riesling from Llano County, Texas, 1988, –89, or –90.

2 tablespoons	Teriyaki sauce
2 tablespoons	Snipped basil
2	Shallots, minced
2 cloves	Garlic, minced
1 tablespoon	Snipped cilantro
1 teaspoon	Minced gingerroot
6 6-ounce	Farm-raised catfish fillets
1 cup	Bran flakes cereal, crushed
¾ cup	Pecan crumbs
¾ cup	Brioche crumbs
1 tablespoon	Ground pepper
	Flour
3	Eggs, lightly beaten
	Clarified butter or virgin olive oil
	Apple-Braised Cabbage *(page 127)*

Combine teriyaki, basil, shallots, garlic, cilantro, and gingerroot. Add catfish and marinate in the refrigerator for 2 hours. Stir together bran flakes, pecans, bread crumbs, and pepper; set aside.

Remove catfish from marinade; dust with flour, dip in beaten eggs and coat with pecan mixture.

Pan sauté fillets in clarified butter or virgin olive oil until golden brown. Finish in 350° oven for 3 minutes. Serve hot with Apple-Braised Cabbage.

SEA BASS IN CABBAGE LEAVES

Serves 6

Try with Graves, Chateau Olivier Grand Cru 1986.

Marinate Sea Bass in Vodka, chives, and pepper for 1 hour in the refrigerator.

Place peppercorns, parsley, bay leaves, clove, mustard seed, and fennel seed in a cheesecloth bag to make a sachet. In a medium stockpot combine sachet, onion, carrot, leek, fennel, and celery root. Add fish stock. Bring to a boil; reduce to slow simmer. Place bamboo steamer over top to season bamboo rack. When vegetables are cooked, strain stock but leave sachet. Purée the vegetables and adjust thickness with fish stock. Set aside. Adjust stock level.

Wrap each fish fillet in cabbage leaves and fold into parcel. Place on bamboo rack. In stockpot combine strained stock, orange juice and zest, and lemon juice and zest. Cover and steam fish over citrus and vegetable broth. Cook gently over low heat for about 8 minutes.

Place a small amount of vegetable purée on the plate. Place bass on top and serve at once.

6 5-ounce	Pieces of Black Sea bass, cleaned and skinned
4 tablespoons	Hunters Vodka (Okhotnichya)
1 tablespoon	Snipped chives
	Fresh cracked pepper
10	White peppercorns
4	Parsley sprigs
2	Bay leaves
1	Clove
½ tablespoon	Mustard seed
½ tablespoon	Fennel seed
½ medium	Onion, cleaned and finely diced
½ medium	Carrot, cleaned and finely diced
½	White leek, cleaned and finely diced
½	Fennel bulb, cleaned and finely diced
½ medium	Celery root, cleaned and finely diced
4 quarts	Fish stock
12	Nappa cabbage leaves (pre-blanched in salted water)
	Juice and zest of 1 orange
	Juice and zest of 1 lemon

MAHI-MAHI STEAK WITH SAN SABA BUTTER SAUCE

Serves 4

Try with San Saba Cabernet Sauvignon 1987—which also adds a special touch to the butter sauce.

2 tablespoons	Snipped lemon-thyme leaves
1 tablespoon	Snipped opal basil
1 clove	Garlic, minced
1 teaspoon	Freshly cracked white pepper
4 7-ounce	Boneless Mahi-Mahi steaks
	Olive oil

Combine thyme, basil, garlic, and pepper; rub evenly into the Mahi-Mahi. Cover and marinate overnight in the refrigerator.

Pan sauté Mahi-Mahi in olive oil over high heat. Sear both sides until evenly golden brown. Remove from skillet and place on platter. Place in oven for 3 minutes. Serve with San Saba Butter Sauce.

SAN SABA BUTTER SAUCE

Place wine, stock, vinegar, and shallots in saucepan and reduce over moderate heat. Add crème fraîche. When mix comes to a boil, reduce heat and whisk in diced butter until totally incorporated into the sauce. Season with a little salt and freshly cracked pepper. Serve with seared Mahi-Mahi.

6 tablespoons	San Saba Cabernet Sauvignon or dry red wine
⅓ cup	Fish stock
3 tablespoons	Rice wine vinegar
1 teaspoon	Chopped shallots
2 tablespoons	Crème fraîche
6 tablespoons	Butter, diced
	Salt and freshly cracked pepper

TILAPIA WITH BRAISED LEEKS AND TOMATO TARRAGON SAUCE

Serves 4

Tilapia, or St. Peter's fish, is widely eaten in the Far East, where it is caught wild. It now is farmed in several states—including Florida and Arizona—in the United States and is readily available in fine local supermarkets. A suggested wine is Duckhorn Sauvignon Blanc 1989.

1½ tablespoons	Butter
2	Shallots, finely chopped
¼ cup	Fish stock
¼ cup	Dry white vermouth
½	Lemon, juiced
	Freshly cracked pepper
4 7-ounce	Tilapia fillets (or red snapper, grouper, or sea bass fillets)

Preheat oven to 350°. Brush a casserole dish with butter and sprinkle with shallots. Add stock, vermouth, lemon juice and cracked pepper. Place tilapia on top; cover with buttered parchment paper and place in oven for 5 to 6 minutes. Reserve fish drippings for Tomato Tarragon Sauce.

BRAISED LEEKS

Melt butter in saucepan. Add stock and leeks. Bring to a boil; reduce heat and steep for 15 minutes or until leeks are tender. Season with nutmeg, salt, and pepper.

1 teaspoon	Butter
1½ cups	Fish or chicken stock
1 pound	Leeks, cleaned, washed, and diced
¼ teaspoon	Ground nutmeg
	Salt and pepper

TOMATO TARRAGON SAUCE

Melt butter in sauté pan. Add shallot and cook for 3 minutes. Add tomatoes and cook for 5 more minutes over low heat. Purée in blender, then bring to a boil. Stir in fish stock, tarragon, salt, and pepper. Before serving, add a dash of vermouth and any fish drippings. Serve tilapia on top of leeks and surround with sauce.

¼ cup	Butter
1	Shallot, finely chopped
8	Ripe tomatoes, peeled and seeded
⅓ cup	Fish stock
2 tablespoons	Snipped fresh tarragon leaves
	Salt and freshly cracked pepper
	Vermouth

BRAISED LAMB SHANK WITH PARSNIPS, CARROTS, AND RISOTTO

Serves 8

A hearty merlot, such as Matanzas Creek Merlot, Sonoma 1988 Varietal, makes a perfect companion.

8	9–10-ounce Lamb shanks, trimmed
	Salt and fresh cracked pepper
3 tablespoons	Flour
8 tablespoons	Olive oil
4	Medium parsnips, cleaned and diced
4	Medium carrots, cleaned and diced
2	Medium onions, cleaned and diced
1	Medium leek, cleaned and diced
16 cloves	Garlic, peeled
8	Tomatoes, cleaned and diced
4	Bay leaves
1 sprig	Rosemary, needles only
¾ cup	Red wine
2 tablespoons	Tomato paste
2 quarts	Beef or chicken stock
½ bunch	Cilantro, chopped
	Risotto or mashed potatoes

Clean lamb shanks, rinse in cold water and towel dry. Season with salt and pepper and dust with flour. Heat 4 tablespoons of the olive oil in sauté pan and pan-sear shanks until golden brown on all sides. Remove from pan and set aside.

In large stockpot heat remainder of oil and cook parsnips, carrots, onion, leeks, and garlic over low heat for 5 minutes. Add tomatoes, bay leaves, and rosemary. Deglaze pan with red wine. Add tomato paste. Stirring continuously, add stock and cilantro. Place shanks in stock mixture and bring to a boil. Reduce heat and simmer for 2 hours over low heat. Add additional stock if needed. Test meat for doneness (meat should flake off the bone with ease). Place shanks on platter; keep warm.

Remove bay leaves from jus vegetable (stock mixture); season with salt and fresh cracked pepper. Reduce by one-third over high heat. Ladle jus with braised vegetables over shanks and serve at once with risotto or mashed potatoes.

GRILLED LAMB LOIN CHOP WITH PEPPERED PINEAPPLE

Serves 8

A suggested wine is Hogue Cellars Merlot 1989, a rich and fruity merlot from the state of Washington.

In shallow dish place pineapple spears and marinate in vinegar, liqueurs, and peppercorns. Refrigerate, preferably over-night, turning once or twice. Rub lamb chops with a mixture of the oil, lemon thyme, and pepper. Grill lamb chops on moderate grill about 10 minutes or till medium, turning several times. Place on serving platter and keep warm. Remove pineapple from marinade and grill on both sides for even markings. Serve at once with lamb chops.

1 medium	Pineapple, peeled, cored, and cut into spears
¼ cup	Raspberry vinegar
2 tablespoons each	Grand Marnier, Galliano, and Triple Sec
2 tablespoons	White peppercorns, crushed
8 7-ounce	Lamb chops, center cut (frenched)
1 teaspoon	Olive oil
1 teaspoon	Lemon thyme
½ teaspoon	Ground black pepper

PAN-SEARED DUCK BREAST WITH RED CURRANT SAUCE

Serves 6

When you caramelize the sugar for the sauce, take extreme care due to the heat. Stir gently and when sugar starts to turn brown, watch it closely to prevent burning. Burning the sugar will make the sauce taste bitter.

Try with Calera, Jensen Vineyard, Pinot Noir 1989.

6 6-ounce	Boneless duck breasts
3 tablespoons	Sugar
3 tablespoons	Butter
1 cup	Chicken stock
½ cup	Red wine (preferably Merlot)
1	Shallot, cleaned and minced
5 tablespoons	Red currants
3 tablespoons	Lingonberry jam
1 teaspoon	White peppercorns, cracked
	Salt and pepper
2 tablespoons	butter, softened
½ tablespoon	Chopped parsley

For sauce, in medium saucepan melt 3 tablespoons butter; add sugar. Cook and stir till sugar caramelizes. Add chicken stock, red wine, and shallot; bring to a boil. Add currants, lingonberry jam, and peppercorns. Reduce heat and simmer gently for 15 minutes over low heat. Season with a little salt and pepper. Stir in 2 tablespoons butter and chopped parsley. Keep warm. Sauce should have a silky, velvet appearance and coat the back of a spoon.

Season duck breasts with a little salt and pepper. In sauté pan sear duck breast, skin side down, till brown (this will alleviate excess duck fat). (Store excess duck fat in small jar in refrigerator for future use in sausage or confit preparation.) Pre-heat oven to 375°. Place duck in saucepan, skin side down, and roast for 15 to 20 minutes or till done. Check occasionally. Remove from oven (save excess fat). Place duck breasts on serving platter and serve with sauce.

PHEASANT PARCEL IN PHYLLO

Serves 12

A suggested wine is Puligny Montrachet (Burgundy) Olivier Le Flaive 1987.

In a skillet melt butter. Add Parma ham and cook for 2 minutes. Add yellow pepper, leeks, shallots, and garlic. Sauté over low heat for 3 minutes. Add corn kernels and mushrooms; combine thoroughly. Add Vermouth and deglaze. Add cooked wild rice, basil, and cilantro. Cook slowly over low heat. Stir mixture carefully. Adjust seasoning with salt and pepper. Heat thoroughly. Cool mixture on baking sheet. Fold Asiago cheese into mixture. Set aside. Under plastic wrap, pound pheasant breast gently with a meat mallet. Do not tear the meat. Sprinkle with fresh cracked pepper. Place equal amounts of the Asiago cheese mixture in center of each pheasant breast. Fold into individual parcels.

Cut phyllo sheets in half. Use 4 half-sheets per pocket. Brush each sheet with clarified butter, layering one on top of the other. Place pheasant in center of phyllo stack. Wrap phyllo around meat to make a parcel. Brush with clarified butter.

Place on a baking sheet and bake in 350° oven for 12 to 15 minutes. Remove from oven. Serve at once with Green Lentil Compote and Green Apple Tomatillo Sauce.

6 tablespoons	Butter
4 ounces	Lean Parma ham, diced
4 tablespoons	Diced yellow pepper
4 tablespoons	Diced leeks
2 tablespoons	Diced shallots
3 cloves	Garlic, minced
6 tablespoons	Fresh corn kernels
6 tablespoons	Fresh Porcini mushrooms, diced
4 tablespoons	Vermouth
1 cup	Cooked wild rice
1 tablespoon	Basil
1 tablespoon	Cilantro
	Salt and pepper
4 tablespoons	Grated Asiago cheese
12	5-ounce Pheasant breasts, deboned, cleaned, and skin and sinew removed
24 sheets	Phyllo dough
	Clarified butter
	Green Lentil Compote *(page 91)*
	Green Apple-Tomatillo Sauce *(page 59)*

GINGERED CHICKEN RAGOUT WITH LINGUINE AND BEAN SPROUTS

Serves 8

I serve this with 1990 Caymus Conundrum.

6 tablespoons	Peanut oil
2	Red onions, finely diced
1 stalk	Leeks, diced
1 stalk	Celery, diced
1 tablespoon	Minced fresh gingerroot
4 cloves	Garlic, minced
1½ quarts	Chicken stock
3	Bay leaves
2 teaspoons	Salt
1 teaspoon	Crushed white peppercorns
2	Whole chicken fryers (about 6 pounds total), washed and cleaned
2	Red peppers, cleaned and diced
2	Yellow peppers, cleaned and diced
1 cup	Bean sprouts
1 pound	Linguine, cooked and rinsed

In large stockpot heat oil and cook onions, leeks, celery, gingerroot, and garlic over low heat. Add chicken stock. Slowly bring to a boil. Add bay leaves, salt, and peppercorns.

Cut fryers into 8 pieces each. Place into stock mixture and simmer gently for 45 minutes. Remove from heat. Remove chicken and cool. Remove skin and meat from bone. Place red and yellow peppers into stock and bring to a boil; add chicken pieces. Heat thoroughly. Adjust seasoning with salt and pepper. Keep warm.

Wash and clean bean sprouts. Place onto a large serving platter. Season cooked linguine with a little peanut oil, salt, and pepper. Place on platter. Place chicken pieces on top and pour hot stock over chicken. Serve at once.

SMITHFIELD HAM AND LEEK TART

Serves 4 to 6

Serve with Mushroom, Roast Garlic, and Artichoke Salad (p. 108).

In large sauté pan heat butter and add ham and bacon. Mix well and cook for 2 minutes over medium-low heat. Add leek and onion and sauté for 3 minutes or until vegetables are tender. Season with salt and white pepper. Cool.

In a large bowl combine eggs. Add heavy cream and sour cream; mix well (do not whip). Add cheeses and mix well. Let rest for 5 minutes. Bake in tart shell at 375° for 30 minutes or till firm to touch. Remove from oven and let cool.

1 tablespoon	Clarified butter
4 ounces	Smithfield ham, diced
3 ounces	Bacon, diced
½ cup	Leek, diced
½ cup	Onion, diced
	Salt
	White pepper
2	Eggs
½ cup	Heavy cream
½ cup	Sour cream
½ cup	Grated Gruyère cheese
½ cup	Grated Monterey Jack cheese
1	9-inch tart shell, baked

Oven-roasted Plum Tomato Soup with Cumino, Coriander, and Avocado Purée with Speckled Cornbread Muffins

Sweetwater Prawns with Parma in Phyllo with Papaya-Tomato Relish

Smithfield Ham and Leek Tart with Mushroom, Roast Garlic, and Artichoke Salad

Rigatoni in Wild Mushroom Broth with Parma Ham and Porcini

Pan-seared Lamb Carpaccio with Tuscan Bean Salad

Smoked Chicken and Three Pepper Soup with Baby Corn

Confit of Duck with Young Green Beans and Creamy Vinaigrette

Gingered Chicken Ragout with Linguine and Bean Sprouts

Grilled Pork Medallions with Braised Flageolets, Zucchini, and Squash

Pheasant Parcel in Phyllo with Sweet Red Pepper Purée and Green Apple-Tomatillo Sauce

Fillet of Salmon in Brioche Crust and Porcini Sauce

Pecan- and Bran-crusted Catfish

Lemon-Lime Tart with Fresh Raspberry Sauce

Poached Pinot Noir Pears with Butterscotch Sauce

Mascarpone, Ricotta, and Raisin Strudel with Vanilla Sauce

Chocolate Almond Fudge Cake with Vanilla Sauce

ACCOMPANIMENTS

GINGERED PORK TENDERLOIN SALAD WITH ARTICHOKES, POTATOES, AND CURRY DRESSING

Serves 12

1½ pound	Pork tenderloin
5 tablespoons	Teriyaki sauce
2 tablespoons	Chopped basil
2 tablespoons	Chopped cilantro
1 tablespoon	Grated gingerroot
1 tablespoon	Freshly cracked pepper
1½ teaspoons	Salt
5 tablespoons	Olive oil
3	Potatoes, boiled with skin on
2 tablespoons	Butter
6	Fresh artichoke bottoms, cleaned, washed, and quartered

Trim pork and cut into ½ inch strips. Marinate pork in teriyaki sauce, basil, cilantro, gingerroot, pepper, and salt for 2 hours in the refrigerator. Drain and sear pork in hot olive oil. Place on baking sheet to cool. Peel, core, and slice potatoes. Heat butter. Sauté quartered artichoke bottoms until evenly browned. Bake in 350° oven until done. Cool. Prepare dressing.

CURRY DRESSING

Combine all ingredients. Toss pork with dressing. Add potatoes and artichokes and combine thoroughly. Refrigerate till serving time. Garnish with Belgian endive, red oak lettuce, and arugula.

Serve with crusty rolls.

¾ cup	Olive oil
½ cup	Rice wine vinegar
4 tablespoons	Chopped gherkins
3 tablespoons	Chopped parsley
1 tablespoon	Capers, chopped
1 tablespoon	Chopped chives
2	Anchovies, chopped
1 clove	Garlic, minced
1½ teaspoons	Madras curry powder
	Salt
	Freshly cracked pepper

MUSHROOM, ROAST GARLIC, AND ARTICHOKE SALAD

Serves 4 to 6

Serve with Smithfield Ham and Leek Tart.

3 tablespoons	Clarified butter
6	Artichoke bottoms, peeled and quartered
24 cloves	Garlic, peeled
1 pound	Button mushrooms, washed and cleaned
24	Green olives
⅓ cup	Virgin olive oil
2 tablespoons	Rice wine vinegar
1 tablespoon	Chopped fresh basil
1 tablespoon	Chopped fresh chives
	Cracked pepper
	Salt

Heat butter in sauté pan. Sauté artichokes until golden. Finish roasting in oven until done but still firm. Set aside to cool. Repeat procedure with garlic until browned evenly. Sauté the mushrooms and allow them to cool. Combine artichokes, garlic, and mushrooms in a bowl. Add remaining ingredients and marinate for 2 hours. Adjust seasoning.

TOMATO RISOTTO

Serves 8

In medium saucepan heat olive oil and cook shallots and garlic. Add wine and cook till almost dry. Add rice and cook for 1 minute, stirring continuously. Slowly add 1 cup of the stock. Cook until stock is absorbed. Add more stock, 1 cup at a time, and cook until stock is absorbed. Repeat until all stock is used. Cook gently for approximately 15 to 20 minutes. Fold in the cheese and the diced tomatoes. Serve at once with lamb shanks.

¼ cup	Olive oil
2	Shallots, finely chopped
1 clove	Garlic, minced
¼ cup	White wine
1½ cups	Italian rice (preferably Arborio)
4 cups	Chicken stock
¾ cup	Grated Asiago cheese
2	Roma tomatoes, diced

SAVORY POTATO PANCAKES

Serves 4 to 6

5	Potatoes
4	Egg yolks
⅓ cup	Diced ham
2 tablespoons	Chopped chives
2 tablespoons	Chopped basil
	Ground nutmeg
	Salt and pepper
3 tablespoons	Clarified butter

Boil whole unpeeled potatoes in plenty of water till tender. Place potatoes on baking sheet and cool for 1 minute; peel potatoes while still hot. Purée potatoes and add yolks, ham, chives, and basil. Season with nutmeg, salt, and pepper. Mixture should be dry and pull away from the sides of the mixing bowl. Form into patties and sauté in clarified butter until crispy and golden. Keep warm in the oven.

APPLE, ONION, AND POTATO PANCAKES

Serves 6 to 8

In stockpot boil unpeeled whole baking potatoes in plenty of lightly salted water till tender. Drain water and cool potatoes. When cooled, peel and grate potatoes with a cheese grater using the coarse grate. Place in mixing bowl. Stir in grated apple and onion. Season with nutmeg, salt, and pepper. Mold into small patties approximately 3 inches in diameter. Sauté patties in butter until browned evenly on both sides.

3 large	**Baking potatoes**
2 medium	**Golden Delicious apples, peeled and grated**
1 medium	**Onion, peeled and grated**
	Fresh nutmeg, grated
	Salt and pepper
3 tablespoons	**Clarified butter**

SPICY YELLOW CORN PANCAKES

Makes about 16 pancakes

½ cup	Sifted cake flour
2 tablespoons	Chopped cilantro
2 teaspoons	Chopped parsley
½ teaspoon	Cumino powder or ground cumin
½ teaspoon	Salt
½ teaspoon	Cayenne pepper
¼ teaspoon	Baking powder
1 pound	Fresh yellow corn kernels
1	Red onion, finely diced
2 cloves	Garlic, minced
3	Eggs
	Vegetable oil

In mixing bowl combine flour, cilantro, parsley, cumino powder, salt, cayenne, and baking powder. Combine corn, onion, garlic, and eggs; fold into flour mixture.

In a large skillet or wok heat 1-inch of vegetable oil. Form dough into pancake shape and drop into fat; cook until golden brown on all sides. Remove from oil and drain on paper towels. Place on platter and keep hot in oven till ready to serve.

GORGONZOLA POLENTA MOONS

Serves 10 to 12

In heavy saucepan bring water and minced garlic to a rapid boil. Quickly whisk in cornmeal. Lower heat to medium-low and stir constantly with wooden spoon for 20 minutes (mixture should be very stiff). Remove mixture from heat and gradually stir in egg and egg yolk. Return pan to low heat and cook, stirring constantly, for 5 minutes. Add Gorgonzola, Asiago, basil, and thyme, stirring to melt cheeses. Season with salt and pepper.

Grease and lightly dust one 9-inch Teflon pie pan with bread crumbs. Pipe polenta mixture evenly into pie pan. Set in water bath. Cover lightly with greased wax paper or parchment paper and bake in center of oven at 325° for 1 hour. Remove from oven; cool. Invert onto a cutting board and cut into moons with cookie cutter.

2 cups	Water
1 clove	Garlic, minced
1 cup	Yellow cornmeal
1	Whole egg
1	Egg yolk
⅓ cup	Crumbled Gorgonzola
2 teaspoons	Grated Asiago cheese
2 teaspoons	Chopped fresh basil
1 teaspoon	Chopped fresh thyme
½ teaspoon	Salt
1 teaspoon	Ground white pepper
¼ cup	White bread crumbs

LAVOSH

Makes about 24 pieces

¾ cup	Milk
¼ cup	Shortening
3	Egg whites
1 tablespoon	Sugar
1½ teaspoons	Salt
1 pound	All purpose flour, sifted
1	Egg white
1 teaspoon	Water
	Kosher rock salt
	Sesame seeds

Using well method prepare dough. Rest dough. Roll out dough very thin to 1⁄16 inch, and cut into desired shapes. Brush with water and egg whites. Sprinkle with Kosher rock salt and sesame seeds and bake at 350° for 3 minutes, until evenly browned.

SPAETZLE

Serves 6

Whip eggs well; add milk. Fold in flour, parsley, and basil. Mix thoroughly. Let stand for 1 hour at room temperature.

Fill large pot with lightly salted water; bring to a boil. Place colander over pot and pass batter through with a rubber spatula into boiling water. Remove colander and cook pasta, stirring occasionally, for 4 minutes. In clean colander drain pasta and rinse with cold water. To serve, pan-sauté spaetzle in a little butter until golden brown. Season with salt, pepper, and nutmeg.

3	Whole eggs
¾ cup	Milk
1 cup plus 4 tablespoons	Cake flour, sifted
1 tablespoon	Chopped parsley
1 tablespoon	Chopped fresh basil
	Butter
½ teaspoon	Salt
Pinch	White pepper
Pinch	Ground nutmeg

CARAWAY RYE DUMPLINGS

Serves 8

The perfect addition to roast goose or turkey and Apple-braised Cabbage (p. 127).

6 tablespoons	Butter
3 cups	Diced caraway rye bread
3 tablespoons	Chopped shallots
⅓ cup	Milk
3 tablespoons	Chopped parsley
2 tablespoons	Flour
3 tablespoons	Chopped crisp-cooked bacon
	Salt and pepper
	Ground nutmeg
	Browned butter

Heat half of the butter in sauté pan and brown diced bread over low heat on all sides. Remove the bread cubes; add remaining butter and cook the shallots for 3 minutes.

In large mixing bowl combine milk, parsley, and flour. Fold in bread and shallots. Add bacon; season with salt, pepper, and nutmeg. Let mixture stand for 30 minutes. Divide mix into 2 equal parts and roll into a cylindrical shape. Place on a clean, wet kitchen napkin; roll and tie with string. Poach the dumpling roll in boiling salted water for 20 minutes, turning the dumpling roll after 10 minutes. Remove from water. Slice dumpling and serve at once with browned butter.

KASHA

Serves 6

*Kasha, or roasted, hulled buckwheat kernels, is today's new starch.
You can substitute quinoa here.*

I n saucepan combine chicken stock and 3 tablespoons butter. Bring to a boil. In bowl mix kasha and egg white thoroughly. In saucepan add shallots and sauté quickly. Add kasha and egg mixture and cook, covered, over high heat to dry kernels. Add boiling stock to kasha mixture and place over medium heat. Cover tightly and simmer for 10 minutes. Check for tenderness and cook till all liquid is absorbed. Fluff with fork and season with freshly cracked pepper, butter, and a little salt.

2¼ cups	Chicken stock
3 tablespoons	Butter
¼ cup	Kasha (buckwheat kernels)
2	Egg whites
¼ cup	Shallots, minced
	Freshly cracked pepper
	Butter
	Salt

PAN-ROASTED ORZO AND BUCKWHEAT

Serves 6

¼ cup	Dry orzo
1 tablespoon	Butter
¼ cup	Kasha (buckwheat kernels)
2 tablespoons	Egg whites
¾ cup	Chicken stock
1 teaspoon	Chopped shallots
	Freshly cracked pepper
3 tablespoons	Walnut oil
3 tablespoons	Chopped Filberts
	Fresh basil
	Cilantro

Prepare orzo according to package directions or cook orzo in boiling salted water until tender. Drain and rinse with cold water. Set aside. Heat butter in sauté pan. In bowl combine kasha and egg whites. Add the mixture to the hot pan, stirring frequently. Add stock, shallots, and pepper. Bring to a boil. Simmer for 10 minutes or until stock is evaporated. Spread kasha mixture on a baking sheet to cool.

In a sauté pan heat walnut oil and add chopped filberts. Cook until browned. Add Kasha and orzo. Season with salt, pepper, fresh basil, and cilantro.

CREAMED ORZO AND LEEKS

Serves 12

Melt butter in saucepan. Add leeks and cook over medium heat. Add chicken stock and simmer until semi-dry. Add orzo and cream; heat thoroughly. Season with salt, pepper, and nutmeg. Just before serving, fold in Parmesan cheese.

4 tablespoons	Butter
2	Leeks, cleaned and diced
1 cup	Chicken stock
1 cup	Orzo, cooked
⅓ cup	Heavy cream
	Salt
	Pepper
	Ground nutmeg
4 tablespoons	Grated Parmesan cheese

SPECKLED CORNBREAD MUFFINS

Makes 16 to 18 muffins

Be sure that the muffin molds are very hot. Vegelene is a non-stick cooking liquid. Should you wish, you could also use any cooking spray.

1½ cups	Sifted cake flour
½ cup plus 2 tablespoons	Yellow cornmeal
6 tablespoons	Brown sugar
4 tablespoons	Chopped cilantro
4 tablespoons	Chopped parsley
3	Serrano chili peppers, seeded and diced
2 tablespoons	Baking powder
2 teaspoons	Salt
5	Whole eggs
1¼ cups	Water
¾ cup	Canola oil

In a food processor combine flour, cornmeal, brown sugar, cilantro, parsley, peppers, baking powder, and salt. Add eggs, water, and oil. Cover and process for 1 minute. Scrape down sides and repeat, mixing for 1 minute. Place container in refrigerator.

Heat small molds, brush with vegelene and heat at 350° for 5 minutes. Fill with cornbread mixture and bake for 15 minutes. Serve warm with soup and salads.

LEMON THYME POTATO PIE

Serves 8 to 10

In large skillet heat 6 tablespoons of the butter over high heat. Once butter is hot add potatoes. Reduce heat to medium-high, stirring potatoes for 7 minutes or until evenly browned. Add sliced onions, white pepper, and salt. Mix well and cook for 4 more minutes. Add lemon thyme. Adjust taste if necessary. Remove potatoes to large shallow pan. Place pan in preheated 350° oven for 10 minutes, rotating once. Remove potatoes and let stand for 10 minutes.

In medium bowl mix eggs and cream. Do not over mix, this creates too much air in the custard.

Once potatoes have cooled, place in large bowl. Add egg mixture and mix well. Place potato mixture in greased 9-inch pan lined with waxed paper or parchment paper. Smooth top and place greased waxed paper on top. Place on baking sheet with water bath. Place in preheated 300° oven for 50 to 60 minutes or until pie is firm in the center. Remove from oven and let stand 5 minutes before serving.

½ cup	Clarified butter
6	Potatoes, peeled, cut into quarters lengthwise, and sliced ⅛-inch thick
1	Onion, thinly sliced
1 teaspoon	White pepper
½ teaspoon	Salt
3 tablespoons	Snipped fresh lemon thyme
3	Eggs
1¼ cups	Heavy cream

FRESH NASTURTIUM BUTTER

Makes 1 cup

10 tablespoons	Sweet cream butter
1 cup	Fresh nasturtium flowers, shredded
½ medium	Red onion
3 tablespoons	Finely chopped chives
2	Serrano peppers, seeded and finely chopped
	Worcestershire sauce
	Salt

In a mixing bowl, cream butter and add nasturtium flowers, onion, chives, and serrano peppers. Combine thoroughly; season with Worcestershire sauce and a pinch of salt.

Place in parchment paper and roll into cylindrical shape.

Refrigerate until well chilled. Slice and serve.

MAPLE APPLES

Serves 6

Wonderful with pork dishes, especially Sautéed Pork Tenderloin with Lima Bean Mustard Sauce (p. 79).

3 large	Granny Smith apples, peeled, cored, and cut into 6 sections each (18 sections total)
1 cup	Bran flakes cereal, crushed
¾ cup	Pecan crumbs
¾ cup	Brioche crumbs
2	Eggs, lightly beaten
	Flour
½ cup	Maple syrup

Preheat oven to 350°. Dust apples with flour; dip in beaten eggs and then breading. In a heated skillet melt butter and sauté breaded apple sections until evenly browned. Bake in a 350° oven for 4 minutes. Remove from oven and drizzle with maple syrup. Serve with pork.

STEWED SMALL WHITE BEANS

Serves 6

In small stockpot heat olive oil. Cook onions, carrots, celery, bacon, sausage, serrano pepper, and garlic for 5 minutes. Add soaked and rinsed beans. Add stock and bring to a rapid boil. Reduce heat and simmer gently till beans are tender, stirring occasionally. Add cilantro and adjust seasoning with salt and pepper.

3 tablespoons	Olive oil
4 tablespoons	Diced onions
4 tablespoons	Diced carrots
4 tablespoons	Diced celery
1 ounce	Diced bacon
1 ounce	Diced Andouille sausage
1	Serrano pepper
2 cloves	Garlic, minced
6 ounces	Small white beans (soaked overnight in cold water)
3 cups	Chicken stock
1 tablespoon	Chopped cilantro
	Salt and pepper

SWEET RED PEPPER PURÉE

Serves 6

5 large	Red bell peppers
1 tablespoon	Virgin olive oil
⅔ cup	Chicken stock
	Salt
	Pepper

Rub peppers with olive oil. Place on a smaller baking sheet and place in 350° oven to brown evenly. Remove from oven and place hot peppers in bowl. Wrap bowl at once with plastic wrap. Let stand, covered, for 10 minutes. Peel peppers and discard seeds and skin.

Purée peppers in food processor. In small saucepan heat pepper purée; add chicken stock and season with salt and pepper. Do not overcook. Serve at once.

CELERY ROOT PURÉE

Serves 6

Serve with venison, lamb, and other game dishes.

½ pound	Celeriac, finely diced
1 cup	Chicken stock
3 tablespoons	Butter
¼ cup	Crème fraîche
2 tablespoons	Butter
	Freshly ground pepper
	Dash salt

Parboil celeriac in salted water and drain. Melt 3 tablespoons butter in a sauté pan; add diced celery and stock and simmer. Cook slowly over medium heat until soft. Remove from heat and purée in food processor or blender. Reheat the purée and add crème fraîche, 2 tablespoons butter, pepper, and salt.

CELERY ROOT AND ONION PURÉE

Serves 6

This purée goes well with lamb, venison, and other game dishes.

In salted boiling water blanch onions and celery root for 5 minutes. Drain; set aside. Melt 2 tablespoons butter in sauté pan and add onion and celery root. Add chicken stock and simmer over low heat until all liquid is reduced. Purée mixture in blender. Heat cream and remaining butter; fold in the celery root and onion purée. Make sure mixture remains blond and does not color.

½ cup	Thinly sliced onions
½ cup	Thinly sliced celery root
5 tablespoons	Butter
1 cup	Chicken stock
¼ cup	Heavy cream

SPINACH MOUSSE

Serves 8; fills 12 ramekins

As with any vegetable mousse preparation the degree of firmness of the custard will vary somewhat depending on the vegetable. Make sure to squeeze out all excess liquid after blanching the vegetables.

1 pound	Blanched spinach
3	Whole eggs
3	Egg yolks
1 cup	Heavy cream
⅛ teaspoon	Salt
⅛ teaspoon	Pepper
⅛ teaspoon	Ground nutmeg
	Clarified butter

Chop the blanched spinach very fine in a food processor. In mixing bowl combine eggs, yolks, and cream. Season with salt, pepper, and nutmeg; fold into spinach. In ramekin or stainless oyster cup, brushed with a little clarified butter, fill with spinach mixture and place in water bath in 325° oven for 40 minutes. Remove from mold. Serve.

APPLE-BRAISED CABBAGE

Serves 8

Tastes best the following day after a thorough reheating.

Combine cabbage, apples, onion, vinegar, and peppercorns; marinate overnight.

In a large saucepan heat olive oil and cook Parma ham over low heat. Add cabbage mixture and stock and cook slowly over low heat for 40 minutes, stirring frequently. Add lingonberries; season with salt and pepper and simmer for 20 minutes.

2 heads	Red cabbage, thinly sliced
4	Granny Smith apples, cored, peeled, and diced
1	Yellow onion, sliced
⅓ cup	Raspberry vinegar
2 tablespoons	Crushed five peppercorns
2 tablespoons	Olive oil
⅓ cup	Parma ham, diced
1 cup	Chicken stock
5 tablespoons	Lingonberries

DESSERTS

PINK GRAPEFRUIT SORBET

Makes 1 quart

2 cups	Sugar
1	Lemon, juiced
1 cup	Water
3 cups	Freshly squeezed pink grapefruit juice

In a saucepan combine sugar, water, and lemon juice. Cook and stir till sugar becomes syrupy, about 5 to 10 minutes. Cool. Stir in grapefruit juice. Freeze in ice cream maker according to manufacturer's directions.

TEQUILA-LIME SORBET

Makes 1 quart

1¾ cups	Sugar
1 cup	Water
	Zest of ½ lime
1½ cups	Freshly squeezed lime juice
1½ cups	Tequila

In saucepan combine sugar, water, and lime peel. Cook and stir till sugar becomes syrupy, about 5 to 10 minutes. Cool. Stir in lime juice and tequila. Strain to remove lime zest. Freeze in ice cream maker according to manufacturer's directions.

CACTUS PEAR SORBET

Makes about 1½ quarts

In saucepan combine sugar and water. Cook and stir till sugar becomes syrupy, about 5 to 10 minutes. Cool. Stir in cactus pear juice, cantaloupe purée, lime juice, orange juice, and tequila. Freeze in ice cream maker according to manufacturer's directions.

2 cups	Sugar
1 cup	Water
2 cups	Cactus pear juice (no seeds)
½ cup	Cantaloupe purée
1	Lime, juiced
¼ cup	Fresh orange juice
2 ounces	Fresh tequila

ROSEMARY SORBET

Makes 1 quart

2 cups	Sugar
2 tablespoons	Fresh rosemary (leaves only)
1 quart	Water
1	Lemon, juiced

Bring all ingredients to a boil and simmer gently (to avoid bitterness) for 15 minutes. Strain to remove rosemary. Cool. Freeze in ice cream maker according to manufacturer's directions.

CUCUMBER MINT SORBET

Makes 1 quart

2 cups	Sugar
1½ cups	Water
2½ cups	Cucumber purée (peeled, seeded and blended in food processor)
1	Lemon, juiced
1 tablespoon	Finely chopped fresh mint
Pinch	Salt

In saucepan combine sugar and water. Cook and stir till sugar becomes syrupy, about 5 to 10 mintues. Stir in cucumber purée, lemon juice, mint, and salt. Freeze in ice cream maker according to manufacturer's directions.

TOMATO BASIL SORBET

Makes 1½ quarts

Combine water and sugar; cook and stir till sugar becomes syrupy, about 5 to 10 minutes. Cool. Stir in tomato juice and pulp, basil, lemon juice, egg white, pepper, and salt. Freeze in ice cream machine according to manufacturer's instructions until firm. Store in freezer until needed.

1 quart	Water
¼ cup	Sugar
1 pound	Fresh tomato juice and pulp
2 tablespoons	Fresh chopped basil
	Juice of ½ lemon
1	Egg white
	Dash of black pepper
	Dash of salt

TARRAGON SORBET

Makes 1 quart

Combine Armagnac and tarragon; let stand for 2 hours. In saucepan combine sugar and water. Cook and stir until sugar becomes syrupy, about 5 to 10 minutes. Cool. Stir in tarragon mixture and grapefruit juice. Freeze in ice cream maker according to manufacturer's directions.

2 tablespoons	Chopped tarragon leaves
1½ cups	Fine Armagnac
1¾ cups	Sugar
1 cup	Water
1½ cups	Freshly squeezed grapefruit juice

ACTUELLE FRUIT COBBLER

Serves 8 to 10

1 cup	Cake flour, sifted
¾ teaspoon	Baking powder
1 cup	Sugar
2	Eggs
¾ cup	Milk
1 teaspoon	Vanilla
1 teaspoon	Grated lemon or orange zest
1	Apple
1	Pear
2	Oranges
½	Pineapple
½	Mango
1	Banana
½ pint	Fresh raspberries
1 tablespoon	Brown sugar
1 tablespoon	Grand Marnier
½ tablespoon	Ground cinnamon
½ tablespoon	Maple syrup
	Butter
	Sugar
	Sifted powdered sugar
	Vanilla ice cream

For batter, stir together flour and baking powder. Add sugar, eggs, milk, vanilla, and zest. Mix well. Let stand 1 hour in refrigerator.

Clean, peel, and core fruit. Cut into medium dice, except berries. Toss fruit with brown sugar, Grand Marnier, cinnamon, and maple syrup. Marinate for several hours.

Grease a shallow 10-inch flame-proof dish with a little butter. Dust with sugar. Place marinated fruit in dish. Pour batter over the fruit. Bake in 350° oven for 25 minutes. Remove from oven and dust with powdered sugar.

Serve with vanilla ice cream.

GINGERBREAD WITH VANILLA ICE CREAM AND CARAMELIZED SUGAR SAUCE

Serves 12

In saucepan combine molasses, butter, and ½ cup water. Bring to a boil; cool. In a bowl stir together egg and 1 cup sugar. Combine flour, baking soda, cinnamon, gingerroot, cloves, and nutmeg. Add to egg mixture. Stir in mascarpone and molasses mixture. Pour into a greased and floured baking sheet. Bake at 350° for 20 to 25 minutes. Cool.

For sauce, gently caramelize 1 cup sugar; deglaze with ¼ cup water and scotch. Keep in warm water bath. With cookie cutter, cut gingerbread into circles. Top with vanilla ice cream and sauce.

1 cup	Molasses
½ pound	Butter
½ cup	Water
1	Egg
1 cup	Sugar
2¼ cups	Flour
1½ teaspoons	Baking soda
1½ teaspoons	Ground cinnamon
1½ teaspoons	Freshly grated Gingerroot
¼ teaspoon	Ground cloves
¼ teaspoon	Ground nutmeg
1½ teaspoons	Mascarpone
1 cup	Sugar
¼ cup	Water
¼ cup	Scotch
	Vanilla ice cream

MASCARPONE, RICOTTA, AND RAISIN STRUDEL WITH VANILLA SAUCE

Serves 8 to 12

This phyllo strudel won the Athens and Apollo Grand Prize for dessert.

½ cup	Butter
½ cup	Sugar
4	Egg yolks
1½ cups	Mascarpone
½ cup	Ricotta cheese
	Zest of ½ orange
	Zest of ½ lemon
4 tablespoons	Raisins
½	Vanilla bean, scraped
4	Egg whites
3 tablespoons	Cake flour, sifted
16 sheets	Phyllo dough
	Melted butter
½ cup	Roasted almonds, chopped
1 cup	Milk
2 tablespoons	Sugar
2	Eggs
	Powdered sugar
	Vanilla Sauce

For filling, beat butter with 4 tablespoons of the sugar. Add egg yolks, one at a time, beating well after each. Gently stir in mascarpone and ricotta. Fold in orange and lemon zests, raisins, and vanilla. Beat egg whites and remaining sugar till stiff peaks form. Carefully fold egg whites into ricotta mixture. Fold in sifted flour.

Place phyllo dough on clean surface, two sheets next to each other, slightly overlapping. Brush with melted butter and repeat procedure for a total of 4 layers (8 sheets). Dust the top layer with half of the chopped and roasted almonds. Place half of the filling on the layered phyllo and roll into a cylindrical shape. Repeat procedure to form second strudel.

Butter an oven-proof baking dish and dust with flour. Place strudels on dish and bake in 350° oven for 15 minutes.

Meanwhile, to prepare the egg custard, boil milk with 4 tablespoons sugar. Remove from heat and mix the eggs with a little of the hot milk. Fold egg mixture into the hot milk and sugar mixture, stirring continuously.

Pour egg custard over the strudels and bake for 30 to 40 minutes more. Remove from oven and let stand for 5 minutes.

Dust strudels with powdered sugar and cut into even portions. Serve hot with Vanilla Sauce.

VANILLA SAUCE

Makes about 1¼ cups

· *Serve sauce with berries, cakes, and ice cream.*

In a saucepan combine milk, sugar, and vanilla. Heat till milk is scalded (180°). Mix yolks with a small amount of scalded milk; stir to combine. Stir egg yolk mixture into scalded milk mixture. Return to heat and cook slowly till mixture coats back of wooden spoon, stirring constantly. Remove sauce from heat; strain and cool in ice bath.

1 cup	Milk
4 tablespoons	Sugar
4	Egg yolks
⅓	Vanilla bean, scraped

CINNAMON VANILLA SOUFFLÉS

Serves 8

1 cup	Sifted pastry flour
5	Egg yolks
1	Egg
1¼ cups	Milk
6 tablespoons	Sugar
2 tablespoons	Butter
½ teaspoon	Scraped vanilla bean
2	Egg yolks
2 teaspoons	Ground cinnamon
1 teaspoon	Fine sugar
4	Egg whites, beaten

In a bowl mix flour, 5 egg yolks, and egg. In saucepan bring the milk, sugar, butter, and vanilla to a boil. Pour milk mixture into the flour and egg mixture. Combine thoroughly. Return to saucepan and cook for 10 minutes, stirring continuously. Remove from heat and add the 2 egg yolks. Mix thoroughly. Let cool.

Place egg mixture, cinnamon, and sugar in mixing bowl. Combine. Fold in beaten egg whites. Butter and sugar 8 ramekin dishes. Fill dishes three-fourths full. Bake in 400° oven for 10 to 15 minutes. Remove from oven. Gently dust with powdered sugar and serve.

PINEAPPLE BEIGNETS

Serves 8

Stir together vinegar, peppercorns, Galliano, Cointreau, and Grand Marnier. Pour over pineapple spears. Cover and marinate overnight.

Combine buttermilk, beer, eggs and salt. Stir in flour to make smooth batter; fold in beaten egg whites.

Drain pineapple spears; dip in batter. Deep-fry pineapple in hot vegetable oil until evenly browned on all sides. Dust with cinnamon and sugar. Serve with Raspberry Purée.

2 tablespoons	Raspberry vinegar
10	Cracked white peppercorns
1 tablespoon	Galliano
1 tablespoon	Cointreau
1 tablespoon	Grand Marnier
1 large	Pineapple, peeled, cored, and cut into 8 spears
1 cup	Buttermilk
¾ cup	Beer
4	Eggs
⅛ teaspoon	Salt
1½ cups	Flour
3	Egg whites, whipped to stiff peaks
	Vegetable oil
	Cinnamon-sugar
	Raspberry Purée

RASPBERRY PURÉE

Makes about 1 cup

Purée raspberries with electric mixer. Pass through a sieve to remove seeds. Boil sugar with red wine and lemon zest. Add berry purée and cook over low heat for 3 minutes. Serve hot or cold with Pineapple Beignets.

¾ cup	Fresh raspberries
6 tablespoons	Brown sugar
⅓ cup	Red wine
½ teaspoon	Grated lemon peel

CRÈME BRÛLEE IN SPICED COOKIE SHELL

Serves 8 to 12

15	Egg yolks
½ cup	Brown sugar
6 tablespoons	Sugar
1 quart	Heavy cream
1	Vanilla bean, split in half

For crème brûlee, beat yolks, brown sugar, and sugar to a strong hot hollandaise. Keep heavy cream and vanilla bean on to boiling point. Add to hollandaise. Set aside to cool overnight in refrigerator.

SPICED COOKIE SHELLS

1 pound	Unsalted butter, softened
6 tablespoons	Sugar
6 tablespoons	Brown sugar
3	Egg yolks
2 tablespoons	Heavy cream
4½ cups	All purpose flour, sifted
2 tablespoons	Fresh grated gingerroot
1 tablespoon	Ground cinnamon
¼ teaspoon	Ground nutmeg
¼ teaspoon	Ground cloves
¼ teaspoon	Cardamom
	Zest of 1 lemon
	Raspberry Sauce (p. 146), optional

Soften butter and add to sugars, but do not beat. Add yolks, one at a time. Stir in cream, flour, cinnamon, gingerroot, nutmeg, cloves, cardamom, and lemon zest. Cover and refrigerate 1 to 2 hours.

Roll out dough and place in a 4–inch cookie ring. Set on sheetpan, line with paper muffin cups and baking beans. Bake shells in 375° oven for 10 minutes. Remove beans and paper lining. Bake till shells are golden brown. Cool; fill shells with chilled crème brûlee. Serve with Raspberry Sauce, if desired.

SWEET PIE DOUGH

Beat together butter and sugar. Stir in flour, egg, vanilla, and lemon zest. Let rest for 1 hour. Use dough to make simple cookie bases, cookies, and tort linings.

1¼ cups	Butter
½ cup plus 3 tablespoons	Sugar
3⅓ cups	Sifted cake flour
1	Egg
½ teaspoon	Scraped vanilla bean
½ teaspoon	Lemon zest

OMA MUTTI'S DUTCH APPLE TART

Serves 12

This is a favorite recipe from my grandmother.

1 cup	**Butter**
1 cup	**Sugar**
1½ cups	**Sifted cake flour**
4	**Eggs**
1	**Vanilla bean scraped**
1 teaspoon	**Finely shredded lemon peel**
2 pounds	**Granny Smith apples, peeled, cored, and sliced**
4 tablespoons	**Toasted almonds**
⅓ cup	**Apricot jam, heated Sifted powdered sugar**

Place butter, sugar, and 1 tablespoon of the flour in mixing bowl. Mix until creamy. Add egg, vanilla, and lemon peel. Slowly fold in the remaining flour. Butter and flour a 10-inch round cake pan. Place half the batter into pan. Arrange apple slices on top of batter; sprinkle with almonds, add remaining batter. Smooth top. Place on baking sheet and bake in a 375° oven for 45 minutes.

While still hot, brush top of tart with warm apricot jam. Let tart cool. Just before serving, dust with powdered sugar.

RASPBERRY "FLUMMERY"

Serves 8

Boil milk with vanilla bean, lime zest, and orange zest. Strain through a chinois. Place in sauté pan and simmer. Stir in semolina. Cook and stir over low heat; stir in dissolved gelatin. Set aside. Beat egg yolks with sugar until creamy and slowly fold into semolina mixture. Stir until mixture is cold. Fold in the whipped cream. Place mixture into small ramekins or large mold. Place the 1 pint raspberries in center of molds. Refrigerate molds for about 5 hours. To make the sauce, blend 1 pint raspberries with apricot brandy and heavy cream.

3 cups	Milk
1	Fresh vanilla bean, scraped
	Zest of ½ lime
	Zest of ½ orange
½ cup	Semolina
4	Envelopes unflavored gelatin, dissolved in a little water
5	Egg yolks, pasteurized
½ cup	Sugar
1¼ cups	Whipped cream
1 pint	Fresh raspberries

Sauce:

1 pint	Fresh raspberries
⅓ cup	Apricot brandy
⅓ cup	Heavy cream

BANANA NUT MUFFINS

Makes 15 muffins (or 2 loaves)

½ cup	Butter
1½ cups	Sugar
2	Eggs
2 cups	Sifted cake flour
1½ teaspoons	Baking soda
½ cup	Light cream
½ cup	Milk
3	Bananas, mashed
½ cup	Chopped hazelnuts, roasted
1	Vanilla bean, scraped

Beat the butter; add the sugar and beat till well combined. Add the eggs, one at a time, beating well after each. Stir together flour and baking soda. Alternately add flour mixture, milk, and light cream. Fold in the bananas, nuts, and vanilla. Fill muffin cups and bake at 350° for 35 minutes or until firm and golden brown. Or, pour batter into 2 loaf pans and bake at 350° for 50 minutes.

BLUEBERRY COULIS

Makes 1½ cups

Combine sugar and water; cook and stir till sugar dissolves. Bring to boiling. Add blueberries; simmer for 2 minutes. Add lemon juice and Kirschwasser. Blend and strain. Can be thickened with arrowroot if needed.

1¼ cups	Sugar
1 cup	Water
4 pints	Blueberries
	Juice of 1 lemon
⅓ cup	Kirschwasser
	Arrowroot (optional)

RHUBARB PRESERVES

Serves 8

Cut rhubarb into cubes; add sugar and lime juice. Place in medium stockpot and cook until tender. In separate saucepan heat Grand Marnier, wine, and peppercorns. Reduce to semi-dry. Combine with rhubarb mixture. Serve rhubarb preserves with vanilla ice cream or sorbet.

1 pound	Rhubarb stalks (no leaves)
1½ cups	Sugar
2	Limes, juiced
½ cup	Grand Marnier
½ cup	White wine
1 tablespoon	Red peppercorns

LEMON-LIME TART WITH FRESH RASPBERRY SAUCE

Makes 1 tart or 8 servings

8 tablespoons	Sugar
½ cup	Unsalted butter, softened
1	Large egg yolk
1	Vanilla bean, scraped
1 teaspoon	Finely chopped lemon zest
2½ cups	Cake flour, sifted

Filling:

5	Eggs
1	Yolk
1 cup	Sugar
⅔ cup	Heavy cream
2½	Lemons, zest and juice
1	Lime, zest and juice
½ pint	raspberries (may use strawberries)
1 tablespoon	Sugar
	Sifted powdered sugar

Mix sugar, butter, and egg yolk to form pommade. Add vanilla bean and lemon zest; fold in flour. Form dough into ball. Wrap with plastic wrap and place dough in refrigerator for 2 hours.

Grease a 10-inch quiche pan (with removable bottom) or springform pan and dust with flour. Roll out dough onto a floured surface; line quiche pan with dough. Place in refrigerator for 15 minutes. Line shell with dry beans. Bake shell in 325° oven for 10 to 15 minutes. Remove from oven and cool. Remove beans.

For the filling, thoroughly combine eggs, egg yolk, and 1 cup sugar; add cream. Just before baking, add lemon juice, lime juice, and peel. Fill baked shell with filling and bake in 325° oven for 15 to 20 minutes until filling is set. Do not brown. Cool on rack.

In food processor or blender, purée raspberries and tablespoon of sugar. Pass through a fine sieve.

Dust tart with powdered sugar and serve with Fresh Raspberry Sauce.

ORANGE, LIME, AND YOGURT TART

Serves 8 to 12

This tart dough will keep well in the refrigerator.

For filling, place 2 eggs and egg yolks in bowl and mix well (do not whip). Add heavy cream and yogurt. Mix well.

Add 1 cup sugar. Mix well, scraping down the sides of the bowl. Add orange and lime juice. Mix well, scraping down the side of the bowl. Set aside.

For pie shell, mix butter and cup sugar until smooth. Add ½ egg, vanilla, and peel. Mix until smooth. Stir in flour until smooth. Remove dough. Place in refrigerator for 1 hour. Roll out chilled dough. Place into 9-inch tart pan. Place in refrigerator for 30 minutes. Bake in 350° oven for 10 minutes, with weight in middle to prevent shrinking. Remove from oven. Let cool 2 minutes. Remove weight and return tart to oven for 5 minutes. Remove and let cool.

Pour filling into baked pie shell. Bake at 300° for 20 to 25 minutes until tart is firm. Remove and cool.

2	Eggs
2	Egg yolks
⅓ cup	Heavy cream
½ cup	Vanilla yogurt
1 cup	Sugar
1	Orange, zest and juice
2	Limes, juice

Shell:

1 cup	Butter, softened
8 tablespoons	Sugar
½	Egg
½ teaspoon	Vanilla extract
1	Orange, peel finely shredded
1	Lemon, peel finely shredded
2½ cups	Flour, sifted

PAPAYA, RASPBERRY, AND STRAWBERRY COMPOTE

Serves 8

2	Medium papayas, cleaned and scooped into small balls
1 pint	Fresh raspberries
1 pint	Fresh strawberries
½ cup	Orange juice
⅓ cup	Kirsch
⅓ cup	Balsamic vinegar
	Fresh mint leaves
1 pint	Low-fat vanilla yogurt

Toss papayas, raspberries, and strawberries with orange juice and kirsch; set in refrigerator for at least 1 hour. Just prior to serving, add vinegar and mint.

Serve well chilled with vanilla yogurt.

PLUM, PEAR, AND APPLE COMPOTE IN PHYLLO WITH MASCARPONE AMARETTO CREME

Serves 12

In large stockpot combine brown sugar, ¼ cup Amaretto, wine, orange juice, lemon juice, cinnamon, and clove. Bring to a boil. Add apples, pears, plums, raisins, and lemon peel; simmer gently over low heat for 10 minutes. Drain and reserve liquid for later. Cool fruit compote.

Place phyllo sheets on clean surface. Brush with butter. Repeat 3 times with additional sheets (4 sheets total). Do not brush last sheet with butter, instead sprinkle with toasted almonds. Place half of the fruit compote on top and roll into a cylindrical shape. Brush top with butter. Repeat with remaining phyllo and fruit to make 2 strudels. Bake in 375° oven for 8 to 10 minutes or until golden brown. Remove from oven and let rest prior to slicing. Cut on angle; dust with powdered sugar. Stir together mascarpone, ⅓ cup Amaretto, and some liquid from fruit compote. Serve strudel with dollops of mascarpone mixture and the reduced compote liquid poured evenly onto plates and allowed to gel naturally.

⅓ cup	Brown sugar
¼ cup	Amaretto di Saronno
¼ cup	Red wine
2	Oranges, juiced
2	Lemons, juiced
¼ stick	Cinnamon
1	Clove
3	Apples, peeled and coarsely diced
3	Pears, peeled and coarsely diced
12	Plums, pitted and coarsely diced
2 tablespoons	Raisins
½ teaspoon	Grated lemon peel
8 sheets	Phyllo dough
	Clarified butter
6 tablespoons	Toasted almonds
	Sifted powdered sugar
1 cup	Mascarpone
⅓ cup	Amaretto di Saronno

POACHED PINOT NOIR PEARS WITH BUTTERSCOTCH SAUCE

Serves 12

The poaching liquid can be stored in your freezer and used again.

4 cups	Water
4 cups	Saintsbury Pinot Noir wine
½ cup	Orange juice
½ cup	Lemon juice
1 cup	Brown sugar
3	Cinnamon sticks
1 teaspoon	Whole clove
	Caramel or butterscotch sauce

In medium stockpot stir together water, wine, orange juice, lemon juice, brown sugar, cinnamon, and cloves. Bring to boiling. Add pears; reduce heat. Poach pears in simmering liquid for 15 to 20 minutes or till just tender. Do not overcook. Cool pears in the liquid. Serve with caramel or Butterscotch Sauce.

BUTTERSCOTCH SAUCE

Makes about 1 cup

Melt butter in a heavy saucepan. Add brown sugar and cook slowly for 1 minute. Add Grand Marnier and water; bring to a boil. Add cream and simmer gently for 5 minutes. Strain. Serve hot or cold.

6 tablespoons	Butter
¾ cup	Brown sugar
2 tablespoons	Grand Marnier
2 tablespoons	Water
⅔ cup	Heavy cream

HAZELNUT, PECAN, AND MACADAMIA NUT TART

Serves 8 to 12

Pastry:

3 cups	Sifted cake flour
1 cup	Butter, softened
1½ cups	Sifted powdered sugar
4	Egg yolks
¼ teaspoon	Grated lemon peel
1 teaspoon	Water
½	Vanilla bean, scraped

Filling:

1 pound	Sugar
¾ cup	Water
1 cup	Heavy cream
1 cup	Cracked roasted hazelnuts
1 cup	Cracked roasted pecans
1 cup	Cracked roasted macadamia nuts
1	Egg yolk
1 tablespoon	Water
	Sifted powdered sugar
	Butterscotch or vanilla sauce

For pastry, place flour in bowl; make a well in center. Stir together butter, powdered sugar, egg yolks, lemon peel, water, and vanilla. Add to flour. Gradually work into a smooth dough. Set aside.

Combine sugar and water in heavy saucepan. Cook gently until sugar starts to caramelize; reduce heat. Slowly and carefully mix in the heavy cream, a little at a time, until mixture is smooth and sugar is dissolved. Add nuts; combine thoroughly and place in shallow dish to cool. Brush an 8-inch springform pan with clarified butter. Dust with flour. Roll out half of the dough. Line springform pan with dough; fill with nut mixture.

Roll out remaining dough. Place on top of nut mixture; fold in edges. Stir together 1 egg yolk and water; brush dough with egg yolk mixture. Prick top of dough with a fork. Rest for 30 minutes. Brush again with egg yolk mixture and bake in 375° oven for 40 to 45 minutes. Remove from oven; rest 10 minutes. Remove from pan; dust with powdered sugar. Serve with butterscotch or vanilla sauce.

POACHED PEAR WITH RASPBERRY YOGURT MINT SAUCE

Serves 6

In a stainless steel saucepan, bring white wine, water, orange juice, lemon zest, orange zest, cinnamon stick, cloves, and vanilla bean to a boil. Reduce to a simmer and add pears. Poach until tender, about 35 minutes. Remove from liquid and cool. Reduce cooking liquid to ½ cup and cool.

Purée 1 pint raspberries with the cooled poaching liquid. Add yogurt and mint. Chill. Serve pears with raspberry yogurt mint sauce.

6	Comice or Bosc pears, peeled
4 cups	White wine
1 cup	Water
	Juice of 2 oranges
1 tablespoon	Lemon zest
1 tablespoon	Orange zest
1	Cinnamon stick
3	Cloves
1	Vanilla bean, scraped
1 pint	Fresh raspberries
3 tablespoons	Plain yogurt
1 teaspoon	Snipped fresh mint

POTTED GINGER CREAM

Serves 8

1 quart	Heavy cream
2	Vanilla beans, scraped
1 cup	Sugar
⅓ cup	Kirsch liquor
2 tablespoons	Grated gingerroot
10	Egg yolks
	Caramel sauce
	Fresh raspberries

Combine cream, vanilla, sugar, kirsch and gingerroot. Place in a heavy double bottom saucepan and scald (180°). Stir a small amount of hot cream mixture into egg yolks. Combine egg yolk mixture and cream mixture; strain. Pour into small ramekins or large ramekin mold. Set into a hot water bath and bake in 300° oven for 20 minutes. Cover container with foil and bake for 20 minutes more. Remove from oven and cool. Serve with caramel sauce and fresh raspberries.

CARROT CAKE "MOUSSIE"

Makes 2 9-inch round cakes

In bowl sift dry ingredients together. In another bowl beat eggs; add oil. Add oil mixture to dry ingredients; mix thoroughly. Stir in grated carrots and chopped pecans, mixing well. Pour mixture into two 9-inch round cake pans, greased and lined with waxed paper. Bake in preheated 300° oven for 50 to 60 minutes or until center is firm. Remove; let stand 15 minutes. Remove from pans when cool.

Beat together the butter and cream cheese. Gradually add powdered sugar and vanilla, beating till smooth. Use to frost carrot cake.

2 cups	Cake flour
2 cups	Sugar
2 teaspoons	Baking powder
2 teaspoons	Baking soda
1 teaspoon	Salt
⅔ teaspoon	Ground cinnamon
4	Eggs
1 cup	Vegetable oil
3 cups	Grated carrots
½ cup	Finely chopped pecans

Frosting:

½ cup	Butter
6 ounces	Cream cheese
1½ cups	Sifted powdered sugar
1 teaspoon	Vanilla extract

WHITE WINE LADYFINGER MOUSSE AND CHAMPAGNE SABAYON

Serves 8 to 10

½	Lemon, juiced
1 cup	White wine (Chateau Montelena Chardonnay)
4	Egg yolks
2 tablespoons	Sugar
2 envelopes	Dry gelatin
4 tablespoons	Warm water
4 cups	Heavy cream, whipped
1	Sponge cake or several ladyfingers
1 small bunch	Seedless grapes Champagne Sabayon Sifted powdered sugar

Combine wine, juice, yolks, and sugar. Heat in double boiler until foamy and stiff. Stir constantly with fine wire whip. Set aside to cool in bowl of ice water. Dissolve gelatin in water; add to cooled egg yolk mixture. Fold in whipped cream. Place ¼ inch layer of cake on bottom and up sides of ceramic mold. Place a few seedless grapes over cake bottom and fill mold with whipped cream mixture. Cool in refrigerator for 3 hours. Spoon 3 tablespoons Champagne Sabayon on each dessert plate. Top with mousse. Sprinkle with powdered sugar.

CHAMPAGNE SABAYON

Makes about 2 cups

1 cup	Dry champagne (Gloria Ferrer-Carneros Cuvee, Brut)
3 tablespoons	Sugar
1	Lemon, peel finely shredded and juiced
10	Egg yolks
2 tablespoons	Kirsch

In the top of a double boiler combine champagne, egg yolks, sugar, Kirsch, lemon peel, and lemon juice. Heat in double boiler, stirring constantly, until foamy and stiff. Serve with White Wine Ladyfinger Mousse.

LADYFINGERS

Makes 24 ladyfingers; serves 8

In mixing bowl combine yolks, half of the sugar, and vanilla; beat until mixture is frothy. In another bowl whip egg whites with remaining sugar to form stiff peaks. Fold cornstarch into the egg white mixture. Add egg yolk mixture to the egg white mixture; fold into the flour.

Pipe batter with a pastry bag using large round nozzle tip onto a cookie sheet. Place ladyfingers 2 inches apart. Bake in 350° oven for 4 to 5 minutes until light gold in color.

6	**Egg yolks**
½ cup	**Sugar**
1	**Vanilla bean, scraped**
4	**Egg whites**
½ cup	**Cornstarch**
⅝ cup	**Sifted cake flour**

SPONGE CAKE

Make 1 9-inch cake

Combine eggs, sugar, lemon peel, and vanilla. Beat with an electric mixer about 10 minutes or until firm and foamy. Gently fold in the sifted cake flour. Fold in the browned butter. Place into a greased and floured 9-inch cake pan. Bake in a 375° oven for 25 to 30 minutes.

5	**Eggs**
⅔ cup	**Sugar**
1	**Lemon, peel finely shredded**
½	**Vanilla bean, scraped**
1 cup	**Sifted cake flour**
4 tablespoons	**Browned butter (beurre noissette), cooled**

BAILEY'S CHOCOLATE RICOTTA MOUSSE CAKE

Serves 12 to 16

7 ounces	Ricotta cheese
5 ounces	Cream cheese
5 ounces	Mascarpone
1 cup	Brown sugar
½ cup	Chopped macadamia nuts, toasted
3 packages	Dry gelatin
⅓ cup	White wine
12 ounces	Semisweet chocolate, melted
¼ cup	Rum
1 cup	Bailey's Irish cream
1 demi-tasse	Espresso
2	10-inch rounds sponge cake, ⅛-inch thick
2 cups	Heavy cream, whipped
6 tablespoons	Raisins
	Butter cream frosting
	Coffee Bean Sauce *(page 165)*

Beat the cheeses and brown sugar in a bowl until soft and fluffy. Add nuts and combine. Dissolve gelatin in white wine. In a bowl combine chocolate, rum and Bailey's; warm to room temperature over a warm water bath. Add coffee and dissolved gelatin; combine thoroughly.

Line a 10-inch mold with sponge cake and brush with Bailey's Irish cream. Fold whipped cream into cheese mixture, then fold in chocolate-rum mixture. Fold in raisins. Pour into mold and smooth top. Cover top with second layer of sponge cake; brush Irish cream. Press until well adhered and refrigerate for 4 hours. Decorate with butter cream frosting. Serve with Coffee Bean Sauce.

BAILEY'S CREME ANGLAISE

Makes about 4 cups

Use a fresh vanilla bean: cut in half, then use the knife point to scrape out the inside.

S cald half the cream and half of the milk in a saucepan with the vanilla bean.

In a bowl, whisk together sugar and egg yolks. Gradually whisk in the scalded cream mixture. Return to the saucepan and add remaining cream and milk. Cook slowly (do not boil) over low heat until the mixture thickens to coat the back of a metal spoon. Strain into container and add Bailey's Irish Cream. Refrigerate before serving.

2 cups	Heavy cream
1 cup	Milk
1	Vanilla bean, knife-point
6 tablespoons	Sugar
6	Egg yolks
½ cup	Bailey's Irish Cream

MOCHA CREAM

Serves 6

2 cups	Milk
¼ cup	Sugar
5	Egg yolks
3 tablespoons	Instant coffee granules
3 tablespoons	Maizena (cornstarch)
2 tablespoons	Kahlua
2 cups	Heavy cream, whipped
	Ladyfingers

Place 1⅔ cups milk and sugar in heavy saucepan. Combine remaining milk with egg yolks and coffee. Scald milk and sugar mixture and stir into the egg yolk mixture. Cook over low heat, stirring continuously, till mixture coats back of a wooden spoon. Combine Maizena and Kahlua; fold into coffee mixture. Cook gently to form cream. Transfer to large bowl and cool. When cool, fold in whipped cream. Spoon into bowls and serve with ladyfingers.

COFFEE BAVARIAN CREAM WITH FRANGELICO SAUCE

Serves 6 to 8

Scald the milk. Whisk the egg yolks and sugar until very light in color. Add Tia Maria and espresso. Pour the hot milk in a thin, steady stream into the egg yolk mixture, whisking gently to combine. Strain the mixture back into a saucepan and cook over low heat. Stir constantly with a wooden spoon until the mixture thickens. Do not boil. Transfer to a bowl over ice. Dissolve gelatin in warm water and add to the hot egg yolk mixture. Cool the mixture, stirring occasionally, until mixture thickens.

Whip cream to stiff peaks and fold whipped cream into the egg yolk mixture. Fill molds and chill until set.

For Frangelico sauce, use Creme Anglaise flavored with Frangelico liqueur. (See Bailey's Creme Anglaise on p. 159 and use ½ cup Frangelico instead of the Bailey's.)

2 cups	Milk
5	Egg yolks
¼ cup	Sugar
⅓ cup	Tia Maria
⅓ cup	Espresso
1 tablespoon	Gelatin
2 tablespoons	Warm water
1½ cups	Heavy cream, whipped
	Cream Anglaise

CHOCOLATE PRALINE RAISIN BREAD PUDDING

Serves 12

1 pound	Cinnamon-swirl raisin bread, diced
½ cup	Heavy cream
3 tablespoons	Praline paste
6 tablespoons	Semisweet chocolate chips
6 tablespoons	Brown sugar
	Zest of one orange
½ teaspoon	Vanilla essence
½ cup	Bailey's Irish Cream liqueur
⅓ cup	Dark rum
6 tablespoons	Raisins
4	Eggs
1½ cups	Whole milk
	Bailey's Creme Anglaise *(page 159)*

Place raisin bread in large mixing bowl. In another bowl combine cream and praline paste and whisk gently until smooth. Add chocolate chips, brown sugar, essence, and orange peel. Stir. Add Irish cream, rum, and raisins. Fold cream mixture into the raisin bread.

In a bowl whisk eggs loosely while adding the milk. Fold into the bread mixture. Combine thoroughly and place mixture in refrigerator for 30 minutes.

Grease a 9½ × 2-inch Teflon cake pan with vegelene (non-sticking cooking liquid). Fill with bread mixture.

Bake in 350° oven for 50 minutes. Remove from oven and cool.

To serve, reheat in microwave oven for 40 seconds on 100% power (high) per portion.

Serve with Bailey's Creme Anglaise.

DOUBLE SIN CHOCOLATE CAKE

Serves 8 to 12

M elt 1 pound chocolate; fold in butter. Beat eggs and sugar and gradually add to chocolate mixture. Fold in flour and white chocolate chunks. Pour into 4-inch greased molds or baking rings. Bake at 400° for 8 minutes.

Scald cream; add 8 ounces chocolate and combine well. Cool. Use as topping on cake.

1 pound	Dark chocolate
10 tablespoons	Unsalted butter, cubed
4	Eggs
2 tablespoons	Sugar
3 tablespoons	All-purpose flour
4 ounces	White chocolate chunks

Ganache:

½ cup	Heavy cream
8 ounces	Dark chocolate

CHOCOLATE ALMOND FUDGE CAKE

Serves 12 to 16

8	Egg yolks
½ cup plus 2 tablespoons	Sugar
1	Vanilla bean, scraped
¾ cup	Sifted cake flour
6 tablespoons	Almond powder
8	Egg whites
6 tablespoons	Sugar
2½ ounces	Semisweet chocolate, melted
½ cup plus 2 tablespoons	Beurre noisette (brown butter), room temperature
	Kahlua
	Chocolate Filling
	Chocolate Glaze
	Coffee Bean Sauce

Place egg yolks in a mixing bowl with ½ cup plus 2 tablespoons sugar and whip over double boiler until mixture reaches body temperature. Continue to beat mixture to a full, thick consistency; add vanilla.

Stir together flour and almond powder. Beat egg whites with 6 tablespoons sugar to form stiff peaks. Slowly fold flour mixture into the egg yolk mixture. Fold in the chocolate and then the beurre noisette. Combine gently as to retain the air in the mixture. Fold in the beaten egg white mixture.

Place mixture into a 10-inch greased and parchment-lined cake pan and bake in a 350° oven for 20 to 25 minutes till cake tests done.

Turn cake out onto a sugared surface. Do not remove the parchment paper; cool. Wrap in plastic wrap and place in refrigerator.

To assemble, slice cake into three even layers, sprinkle each layer with Kahlua and spread with Chocolate Filling. Place layers on top of each other and glaze with Chocolate Glaze. Serve with Coffee Bean Sauce.

CHOCOLATE FILLING

Makes about 2 cups

8 ounces	Bittersweet chocolate
2 tablespoons	Sugar
1 cup	Heavy cream
2 tablespoons	Butter

Cut chocolate into small pieces and place in mixing bowl. Combine sugar and cream in a saucepan and bring to a boil. Pour mixture over chocolate and stir until chocolate has melted. Stir in butter until well combined (do not get mixture too hot or the butter will separate).

Store in a covered container in the refrigerator. Use to fill Chocolate Almond Fudge Cake.

CHOCOLATE GLAZE

Makes about 2½ cups

Cut chocolate into small pieces. Place in double boiler over barely simmering water. Cook and stir till chocolate melts. Stir in butter and syrup. Be careful not to overheat. Set aside.

Whisk together cream, grappa, and cocoa powder. Fold into chocolate mixture till well combined. Spread over cake while glaze is still warm.

9 ounces	Sweet chocolate
5 tablespoons	Butter
1 tablespoon	Maple syrup
¾ cup	Heavy cream
4 tablespoons	Grappa
2 tablespoons	Unsweetened cocoa powder

COFFEE BEAN SAUCE

Makes 6 cups

This sauce—which stores well—is perfect with a large tart.

Stir together sugar and cornstarch in large heavy saucepan. Add milk. Scrape vanilla beans into milk mixture and heat to just scalding. Stir a little warm milk mixture into yolks and add yolk mixture to saucepan. Heat slowly, stirring constantly, to scald (180°) or until mixture coats a wooden spoon. Remove from heat immediately and strain. Add vanilla bean back to mixture. Stir in espresso.

Cool rapidly in an ice bath, stirring often. Chill till serving time.

2 cups	Sugar
1 teaspoon	Cornstarch
4 cups	Milk
1	Vanilla bean, split
25	Egg yolks
½ cup	Espresso

SHORTBREAD COOKIES

Makes about 24 to 30 cookies

¾ cup plus 2 tablespoons	Sugar
1½ cups	Butter
6	Egg yolks
3 cups	Sifted cake flour
1	Lemon, peel finely shredded
Dash	Salt
	Vanilla extract
1	Egg
1 teaspoon	Water
	Sugar

Mix sugar and butter by hand to form pommade. Fold in egg yolks, flour, lemon peel, salt, and vanilla to make dough; refrigerate 1 hour. Roll out dough to ⅙-inch thick. Cut with desired cookie cutters. Stir together egg and water; brush over cookies. Sprinkle with sugar. Bake at 325° until golden brown.

HAZELNUT COOKIES

Makes about 24 to 30 cookies

These delicate cookies are perfect with after-dinner espresso.

1 cup plus 2 tablespoons	Sugar
1¼ cups	Butter
2½ cups	Sifted cake flour
2	Eggs
½ cup	Cornstarch
1 cup	Coarsely chopped hazelnuts
½	Lemon, peel finely shredded
½ teaspoon	Vanilla essence
Dash	Salt

Knead sugar and butter by hand to form pommade. Stir in flour, eggs, cornstarch, nuts, lemon peel, vanilla essence, and salt. Form into a brick shape, cover in plastic wrap, and let stand overnight in the refrigerator. To bake, cut into ¼-inch thick slices and bake at 325° oven for 5 to 7 minutes until a nice golden brown.

HIPPENMASSE

Makes about 24 cookies

Hippenmasse *are very fine almond paste cookies. Can be made with or without a cookie template.*

Mix together almond meal, sugar, flour, cream, milk, vanilla essence, and cinnamon to form a paste with no lumps. Beat together egg whites and powdered sugar till stiff peaks form. Fold paste into egg white mixture, a little at a time.

Drop batter onto greased and floured baking sheet. Bake at 325° until golden brown.

1 cup	Fine almond meal
1 cup plus 2 tablespoons	Sugar
1 cup	Sifted cake flour
½ cup	Heavy cream
2 tablespoons	Milk
⅛ teaspoon	Vanilla essence
⅛ teaspoon	Ground cinnamon
3	Egg whites
1 cup	Sifted powdered sugar

ALMOND CRISPS

Makes about 24 to 30 cookies

In saucepan combine sugar and butter; place over heat till butter melts. Stir in flour, egg, almonds, vanilla, and salt. Form into a brick shape, cover with plastic wrap, and let stand overnight in the refrigerator. To bake, cut into ¼-inch thick slices and bake in 325° oven for 5 to 7 minutes until a nice golden brown.

1½ cups plus 2 tablespoons	Sugar
1⅛ cups	Butter
3¾ cups	Sifted cake flour
1	Egg
1 cup	Sliced almonds
½ teaspoon	Vanilla extract
Dash	Salt

ALMOND HAZELNUT STICK COOKIES

Makes about 24 cookies

1¼ cups	Brown sugar
1 cup	Finely chopped almonds, roasted
½ cup	Finely chopped hazelnuts, roasted
⅓ cup	Heavy cream
12 sheets	Phyllo dough
⅓ cup	Clarified butter
½ cup	Mascarpone, whipped until spreadable
	Sifted powdered sugar

In mixing bowl combine brown sugar, almonds, and hazelnuts. Stir in the cream (mixture may be somewhat pasty, but not soft).

On clean work surface, spread 1 sheet of phyllo dough; brush evenly with clarified butter. Place 1 more sheet on top.

Spread one-sixth of the mascarpone and one-sixth of the nut mixture over phyllo. Roll into a tight cylinder shape; brush with clarified butter. Repeat procedure with remaining phyllo, mascarpone, nut mixture, and butter. Bake in 350° oven till golden brown. Remove from oven. Cool slightly; dust with powdered sugar and cut into slices. Serve with pudding or as a snack.

SOUTHERN COMFORT EGGNOG

Serves 6

Beat egg yolks, sugar, and salt until thick and lemon-colored. Stir in rum and Southern Comfort. Fold egg yolk mixture into whipped cream. Beat egg whites until stiff and gently fold into egg yolk mixture. Chill thoroughly. Serve topped with grated nutmeg. Thin with milk, if desired.

4	Egg yolks, pasteurized
½ cup	Sugar
⅛ teaspoon	Salt
4 tablespoons	Rum
4 tablespoons	Southern Comfort
2 cups	Heavy cream, whipped
4	Egg whites
	Grated nutmeg
	Milk (optional)

APPENDICES

Arugula—salad green, slightly bitter in flavor.

Asiago—dry Italian cheese, similar to Parmesan.

Balsamic Vinegar—wine vinegar aged in oak casks.

Batonnets—strips of meat or vegetables about 2″ by ⅜″.

Beurre Blanc (white butter sauce)—white wine, wine vinegar, shallots and garlic are reduced, then cream is whipped in and then butter is folded in.

Blackening—fish or meat is coated in a seasoning mixture containing sandalwood; black, white, and red peppers; salt; and sugar. It is then quickly seared in a white-hot cast iron skillet.

Blanching—cooking vegetables or other foods briefly in a large pot of boiling water to set their color or partially cook them. After blanching the item is quickly immersed in iced water to stop the cooking process.

Bok Choy—Chinese cabbage.

Brangus—crossbreed of Angus and Brahman cattle. Ours is from the Bradley Ranch in Childress, Texas and is raised without hormones or steroids on natural feed.

Brown Stock (Veal Stock)—veal bones are browned in the oven then simmered in water for about 8 hours with roasted leeks, carrots, onions, celery, and aromatics (herbs).

Brunoise—finely diced vegetables, generally cut ¼″ or smaller used in fillings, soups, and sauces.

Calvados—Brandy distilled from apples.

Caraway—Plant whose black seeds are used to flavor certain cheeses and cakes. Taste between aniseed and fennel (liquorice).

Carpaccio—paper-thin slices of raw sirloin. We take a whole sirloin, marinate it for 4 days with shallots, garlic, basil, olive oil, and balsamic vinegar. The sirloin is then seared quickly and chilled.

Celeriac—celery root. Large brown crisp root, white on the inside, fairly strong celery flavor.

Chianina Beef—The Chianina is an Italian breed of cattle, raised for its low fat content. It is a very large breed, standing six feet at the shoulder.

Cilantro—distinctively flavored Mexican herb, in English it is coriander. Frequently used in Mexican, Southwestern and Oriental cookery. Also called "Chinese parsley."

Compote—Preparation of fresh or dried fruits in a thick or thin syrup, flavored or not with various aromatics such as vanilla, lemon or orange zest, cinnamon, cloves, etc.

Concasse—chopped, finely diced.

Confit—Meat of duck (or goose, pork) cooked in its fat and kept covered in same fat to prevent its coming in contact with air. Duck confit—duck legs are marinated for two days with shallots, garlic, thyme, peppercorns, bay leaf, mustard seeds, and salt. The duck fat is removed and rendered to a liquid. The duck meat is then cooked slowly (3 hours) in the rendered fat.

Cucumber "spaghetti"—English cucumber sliced into long noodles in balsamic vinaigrette.

Coulis—liquid purée.

Curing—removing moisture by drying, pickling, smoking, etc.

Crème Fraîche—naturally fermented cream.

Demi-Glace and Glace—Demi-glace is the result of cooking a stock until it is reduced by half; glace is the result of cooking it to a syrup.

Deglaze—after meat has been sautéed or roasted, the pan is degreased and liquid (stock, wine, water, or cream) is added. The browned particles are scraped up and incorporated into the liquid as it cooks.

Duxelles—a mixture of finely chopped mushrooms, shallots, and seasonings sautéed in butter and cream until the liquid is evaporated.

Dilled Salmon (Gravlax)—Norwegian salmon cured with salt, sugar, dill, peppercorns, and brandy. Sometimes we use gin and juniper berries rather than the brandy.

Forcemeat—a mixture of finely chopped and highly seasoned meat, fish, or vegetables used in pâtés, galantines and molds, or served alone.

Frisee—salad green. Very curly, pale green leaf. Also known as curly endive or chicory.

Frizzled Leeks—thin strips of leeks, fried quickly in hot oil.

Gratinee or au Gratin—terms used to describe dishes that have been sprinkled with butter, bread crumbs, and/or cheese and then baked or broiled until brown.

Harlequin—dish composed of "bits and pieces" artfully arranged.

Jicama—Mexican root vegetable. Crunchy, potatolike.

Julienne—food cut into matchlike strips.

Kasha—cooked buckwheat.

Mirepoix—equal parts of coarsely chopped carrots, onions, and celery.

Morel—mushroom. Highly prized, found in spring on the fringe of woods.

Mousse or Mousseline—purée of vegetables, meat, or fish lightened by the addition of whipped cream.

Okhotnichya—Russian vodka flavored with honey and grasses.

Panade—binding agent, usually made from bread and milk.

Pâté—baked, usually darker meats such as game or pork. Sometimes baked in pastry *"en croute"* but not necessarily.

Polenta—Italian in origin, made from yellow cornmeal.

Porcini—pungent mushroom.

Quinoa—wheat hull.

Ragout—ragouts are made from meat, fish, or fowl. Similar-sized pieces are cut and browned, sprinkled with flour, and then stock or meat juices are added.

Reduce—to cook a liquid decreasing its volume by evaporation in order to concentrate its flavor and make a thicker consistency.

Roux—a cooked mixture of butter and flour used as a thickening agent in some sauces.

Saffron—from Spain. The most expensive herb. Intense yellow color.

Sandalwood—aromatic wood; ingredient used in our blackening mix.

Seabean—pousse-pierre, salty, crunchy; from France.

Serrano Chili—small green chili, fiery hot, used in Mexican and Southwestern cookery.

Shiitake—pungent mushroom.

Stock—a liquid in which meat, poultry, fish bones or vegetables and their appropriate seasonings have been cooked; used as a basis for soups, stews, and sauces.

Sweat—to cook food over low heat until it is translucent and glossy without affecting its color.

Sweetbreads—thymus gland, from the throat of young calves.

Tamarillo—from New Zealand. Tree-ripened tomato.

Tarragon—herb often used to flavor salads and dressings.

Tart—pastry filled with fruit, jam, or custard. Usually open or single crusted pie.

Tartare—name given to raw minced beef steak, seasoned and served with capers, and chopped onion. Term can also be applied to other food prepared in same fashion, such as salmon.

Tomatillo—green berry in a husk; not a tomato but still similar to a tart green tomato.

Terrines—"terrine" refers to the mold that these items are cooked in. Usually white meat such as fish or chicken, or else vegetable. Terrines are cooked in a water bath.

Tilapia—fresh water fish farm-raised in Florida. Firm textured and mild flavored, it is a member of the drum family of fish and may be compared to grouper in flavor. Also called St. Peter's fish or Miracle fish it is said to be the fish that Jesus pulled from the Sea of Galilee to feed the five thousand. Tilapia originally came from African waters.

Tortelini—small torteloni.

Torteloni—crescent shaped pasta filled with ricotta cheese and herbs.

Tortilla Soup—traditional Mexican soup with chicken broth and tortillas. Ours is untraditional with a base of smoked duck consommé, crisp tortilla strips, smoked duck, diced tomato, avocado, cilantro, serrano chilies and wild rice.

Vin Blanc—sauce made from butter, mirepoix, fish stock, leeks, mushroom stems, white wine, cream, bay leaf, and peppercorns.

Zest—finely grated citrus peel.

MEASUREMENTS

Liquid Measures

1 cup   = 8 fluid ounces
2 cups = 16 fluid ounces
4 cups = 32 fluid ounces
2 cups = 1 pint
2 pints = 1 quart
1 quart = 4 cups
4 quarts = 1 gallon

One-Pound Equivalents

2 cups butter
4 cups all-purpose flour
2 cups granulated sugar
3½ cups packed powdered sugar
2¼ cups packed brown sugar

Dry Measurements

3 teaspoons   = 1 tablespoon
4 tablespoons = ¼ cup
16 tablespoons = 1 cup
2 tablespoons = 1 ounce
4 ounces   = ¼ pound
16 ounces   = 1 pound
1 pound   = 454 grams

Metric Measurements

1 teaspoon   = 5 milliliters
1 tablespoon = 15 milliliters
1 cup   = 240 milliliters
1 ounce   = 28 grams
1 pound   = 454 grams

INDEX